SUBJECT MENTORING IN THE SECONDARY SCHOOL

Student teachers have always worked with professionals during their teaching practice, but as teacher training becomes more school based, the role of the mentor has become much more important. Even newer is the emergence of the subject mentor.

This book is an examination of the nature of effective mentoring and its contribution to student teacher development. Part I of the book has a broad perspective. It looks critically at policy developments and the differing approaches to teacher education which have been prompted by government and teacher educators. Part II explores central issues which have emerged in the authors' research with mentors. It identifies tendencies in subject mentoring which characterise the work of subject mentors in schools, and key aspects of mentoring are examined, such as collaborative teaching, observation and the practice of discursive mentoring.

James Arthur, **Jon Davison** and **John Moss** are members of staff at Canterbury Christ Church College.

SUBJECT MENTORING IN THE SECONDARY SCHOOL

*James Arthur, Jon Davison
and John Moss*

London and New York

First published 1997
by Routledge
11 New Fetter Lane, London EC4P 4EE

Simultaneously published in the USA and Canada
by Routledge
29 West 35th Street, New York, NY 10001

Typeset in Garamond by
Florencetype Ltd, Stoodleigh, Devon

Printed and bound in Great Britain by
Creative Print and Design (Wales), Ebbw Vale

British Library Cataloguing in Publication Data

A catalogue record for this book is available from the British Library

Library of Congress Cataloguing in Publication Data

A catalogue record for this book has been requested

ISBN 0–415–14892–8

CONTENTS

ACKNOWLEDGEMENTS

The authors gratefully acknowledge the support of the many mentors, student teachers and colleagues who made this project possible. In particular we wish to thank: the mentors who took part in our studies and took time out of their already heavily loaded schedules to respond in depth to our questions; Hywel Jakeway; Richard Dunnill; the Scottish Office Education Department, which provided us with an overview of current trends in Initial Teacher Education; Vivian McIver, Department of Education Northern Ireland; David Reid, University of Manchester; John Savin and colleagues, Manchester Metropolitan University; Alistair McMillen, Queen's University Belfast; Anne Shelton Mayes, Open University; John Howie, Scottish Office Education Department; and Margaret Wilkin, Homerton College, Cambridge, for her comments on early drafts of this book. The authors also gratefully acknowledge the research funding provided by Canterbury Christ Church College, which supported the study of mentoring reported in this book.

ABBREVIATIONS

CATE	Council for the Accreditation of Teacher Education
CNAA	Council for National Academic Awards
DENI	Department of Education Northern Ireland
DES	Department of Education and Science
DfE	Department for Education
DfEE	Department for Education and Employment
EIS	Educational Institute of Scotland
ELB	Education Library Board
GBA	Governing Bodies Association
GTC	General Teaching Council (Scotland)
HEFC	Higher Education Funding Council
HEI	Higher Education Institution
HMCI	Her Majesty's Chief Inspector
HMI	Her Majesty's Inspectorate
ITE	Initial Teacher Education
ITT	Initial Teacher Training
LEA	Local Education Authority
MOTE	Modes of Teacher Education
MSC	Manpower Services Commission
NCATE	National Council for the Accreditation of Teacher Education (USA)
NCC	National Curriculum Council
NCVQ	National Council for Vocational Qualifications
NQT	Newly Qualified Teacher
OFSTED	Office for Standards in Education
PDS	Professional Development School (USA)
PGCE	Post Graduate Certificate in Education
QCA	Qualifications and Curriculum Authority
QTS	Qualified Teacher Status

SCAA	School Curriculum and Assessment Authority
SCITT	School-Centred Initial Teacher Training
SOED	Scottish Office Education Department
TTA	Teacher Training Agency
UCET	University Council for the Education of Teachers

INTRODUCTION

Initial Teacher Education (ITE) has changed significantly over the past five years. The introduction of school-based courses founded upon partnerships between schools and Higher Education Institutions (HEIs) has led to significant changes in the working practices of tutors and teachers involved in teacher education. A major facet of these changes has been the time to be spent by student teachers in school – for example, 120 days out of a 180-day course, some 66 per cent of a secondary PGCE programme. Such a shift in course structure has meant that new systems and new ways of working have had to be developed. Perhaps the most far-reaching innovation in order to facilitate these new practices has been the creation of the role of 'mentor' in schools. The role of mentor has been well established in other areas of the working world, but it is relatively new to education. Even newer, perhaps, is the emergence of the 'subject mentor'.

It is the aim of this book to contribute to the growing body of knowledge about how student teachers develop their knowledge, beliefs, understandings and skills while they are in school and how subject mentoring might most helpfully support their professional development. The main focus of this book, therefore, is upon subject mentoring rather than upon the subject mentor, for while we acknowledge that there are personal skills, qualities and attributes which might be identified as comprising, or indeed exemplifying, a good subject mentor and that positive professional relationships between student teacher and subject mentor are of significance, it is the processes of mentoring which we believe to be of most importance. By processes of mentoring, we do not mean the practices of mentoring (observing student teachers, collaborative teaching, giving feedback, and so on) but rather we refer to the underpinning and unifying approach in which all such activities might be conducted

1

in order to facilitate student teacher development. It is the aim of this book to provide a conceptual framework which will support subject mentors in developing both their student teachers and themselves professionally. At the heart of this book we propose that student teacher development and the processes of mentoring are most productively placed within the dialogue of educational discourses which encompass classroom practice, for, as Stubbs (1983) reminds us, 'language, action and knowledge are inseparable'.

A BRIEF OUTLINE OF THE BOOK

The years 1992–1996 saw a rapid expansion in the literature which mapped the developing field of mentoring, for example the works of Glover and Mardle (1995), Hagger et al. (1993), Kerry and Shelton Mayes (1995), Furlong and Maynard (1995), Stephens (1996), Tomlinson (1995b), Watkins and Whalley (1993), Wilkin (1992) to cite but a few. Given the emergent nature of the concept of mentoring in schools, it is unsurprising that, with a few exceptions, many texts focused in the main upon management issues and practices in mentoring which might contribute to student teacher development. There was less focus on defining the scope of the dialogue which subject mentors in particular need to promote to make such contributions. Many texts during the early 1990s concentrated upon generic mentoring issues, rather than considering the subject-specific dimension of mentoring. Therefore, we undertook a study, in both a theoretical sense and an empirical sense, of mentoring and mentors of PGCE secondary student teachers in the south-east of England between 1993 and 1996. Initially, we wished to uncover what it was that mentors were doing with student teachers; how they were going about these activities; what their rationale was, and what, if any, were the perceived benefits to mentors, student teachers and pupils of mentoring practices described in the literature, such as 'collaborative teaching'. It is the results of our studies, both theoretical and empirical, which underpin this book.

The book has two parts. Part I of the book has a broad perspective and looks at policy developments in ITE and examines the approaches to ITE which have been promoted by government and its teacher education-related agencies, and by teacher educators throughout the United Kingdom. The first four chapters, which consider policy, assessment, professional values and teacher development, in the main draw on our earlier and theoretical studies, whereas the practice-based Part II focuses predominantly upon our work carried out during 1995–1996. Chapters 5, 6, 7 and 8 draw upon the results of our study of mentors and discuss key aspects of mentoring. While some readers more concerned with the practices of mentoring might wish to go straight to this section, the models of mentoring and of student teacher development, which are assumed in Part II, have their rationale in Part I of the book.

PART I

We begin in Chapter 1 by examining recent policy developments in the United Kingdom. First, we place the current classroom context in England and Wales within the paradigms of policy which have emerged in recent years and note that the development of government policy has been characterised by: the absence of dialogue between policy makers and educationists; the influence of the 'New Right' and its discourse of *apprenticeship*, which sees teaching as a craft; the proposal for, and construction of, teacher education courses based on a competence model of development – a model which purports to be context-free and value-free. The chapter argues that the central feature of the changes in ITE in England and Wales is that they have been centrally devised and imposed and are the result of a coherent political ideology. However, the chapter also traces the development of teacher education policy in Scotland and in Northern Ireland in recent years and shows that substantially different models have been proposed, or have emerged.

Chapters 2 and 3 consider the implications for mentors in respect of assessment and professional values. Chapter 2 considers approaches to assessment in the light of the currently dominant discourse. In particular, it notes how interpretation of competency-based models of teacher development can put the emphasis on the development of the *teacher-as-technician* and ignore what Hopkins (1996) calls 'the moral purpose of education'. The chapter calls for a clear policy on assessment, which stimulates and encourages all-round professional development of student teachers, and which bases competences upon a solid foundation of explicated professional values. Chapter 3 explores the concept of professional values and notes the absence from the current dominant discourse of the value dimension of teaching and its tendency to deprofessionalise not only the teacher, but also the teacher educator. The chapter endorses the 'need to acknowledge the value dimension in educational practice, the fact that it is

3

always a matter of choices, and that those values and those choices are not objects of a scientific or positivist form of study, but are far more problematic than that, so that they need to be approached without dogmatism and with a genuine openness' (Kelly, 1995: 136).

Chapter 4 considers models of student teacher development. It notes the dichotomy which is apparent between those who see teacher development as primarily concerned with the acquisition of skills and those who have made the case for the development of 'reflective practice'. The chapter explores the cases made for and against the role of 'theory' in learning to teach and highlights the existence of competing models and conceptions of the reflective practitioner. The central theme of the chapter is that student teacher development is more complex than many models would suggest – particularly those which describe it as a straightforward journey from novice to expert.

PART II

Part II of the book draws upon our study of mentors of PGCE secondary student teachers in the south-east of England between 1993 and 1996. Chapter 5 gives details of the study and identifies tendencies in subject mentoring which characterise the work of mentors in the study. The chapter proposes that two main tendencies in mentoring may be identified – pragmatic and discursive – and goes on to examine practices which characterise these approaches.

In the light of the discussion in Part I of the book and based upon evidence from our study, Chapter 6 proposes that teacher development takes place through a *dialogue of educational discourses*. There is now a body of literature which has documented very clearly the skills, qualities and attributes of the mentor – although much of this literature focuses upon policy development, or generic mentoring. Similarly, as well as a body of commercially produced texts of mentoring practices, HEIs have produced a wealth of material to support teachers in schools undertaking the role of the mentor. What has been absent hitherto has been an attempt to define the dialogue in which subject mentor and student teacher engage when developing *reflection* – which, as many have noted, is a practice that has been conceptualised in many different ways. While much has been written about levels of criticality in reflection, little has been produced to make explicit the nature of the dialogue through which reflection and teacher development are stimulated. We realise, of course, that the widespread practice of subject mentoring in schools is still in its early stages and understandings of the processes involved in mentoring are still growing and will continue to grow in coming years. The discussion of mentoring in this chapter is presented in the hope that it will further the understanding of the processes of subject mentoring for mentor and tutor alike, and suggest further areas for research.

Chapter 7 uses data gathered in the study of mentors and a case study of a student teacher's classroom practice to exemplify our proposed model of the dialogue of educational discourses within which student teacher development takes place. The chapter explores a key practice now central to, and common among, many HEI courses: collaborative teaching. The case study of a collaboratively taught English lesson is analysed, identifying the educational discourses, described in Chapter 6, which discursive subject mentoring can access.

Finally, Chapter 8 draws together the themes explored in both parts of the book. The chapter argues that in school-based ITE, subject mentors can play a key role in developing teachers who have the capacity to theorise from practical experience, particularly if they adopt the practices of discursive mentoring. However, discursive mentoring cannot easily be introduced and sustained by individual mentors on their own. Therefore, the chapter explores the ramifications of discursive mentoring for the school and the implications of discursive mentoring for the subject department. The role of the 'learning school' in supporting subject mentoring is discussed with reference to the concept of the Professional Development School that has been influential in the USA. Ultimately, possibilities are considered not only for the development of student teachers, but also for their colleagues through a dialogue of educational discourses within the 'mentoring school' and the 'mentoring department'.

Part I

THE CONTEXTS OF SUBJECT MENTORING

1

THE DEVELOPMENT
OF POLICY

INTRODUCTION

A salient feature of developments in Initial Teacher Education (ITE) over the last decade has been the rise of mentoring and competency-led models. This chapter examines these models, their origin and growth, and their impact upon teacher education. The models have their beginning in the USA, but have spread to all parts of the United Kingdom. As seen below, however, the speed and extent of their introduction have varied significantly in different areas of the United Kingdom, as has the response of established teacher education provision. An examination of these differences is vital in determining the wider context of current provision and developments.

A REVIEW OF ITE IN ENGLAND AND WALES

The central feature of development in ITE since 1979 in England and Wales is that it has been centrally devised and imposed as the outcome of a coherent political ideology. This is a new, and, many would say, sinister development in English educational history. In the absence of a General Teaching Council for England and Wales coupled with the diversity of unions representing the teaching profession, it is clear that the teacher's voice in these major changes has largely been ignored. Teachers have witnessed the removal of their bargaining rights, the imposition of contracts with defined hours of work, and the introduction of appraisal, graded inspections, the National Curriculum and national testing with school league tables. In addition, it could be said that teacher education has been subject to more State agencies than any other type of educational activity.

Throughout the 1980s the political Right sought to transform teacher education into an entirely school-based apprenticeship and with this influence and aim in mind the scale of government intervention has increased dramatically. Wilkin (1992) argues that it was an attempt to challenge the autonomy of the teaching profession, but one might ask 'what autonomy?' As Lawton (1994: 109) concludes in his commentary on teacher education: 'The Tory Mind ... distrusts many kinds of professional expertise, prefers learning by experience to theory, and is particularly suspicious of education theory and its use as part of the education and training of teachers.' He suggests that the government's intention is to separate teacher education from the rest of higher education in order to make teacher training more like a school-based apprenticeship. There are many right-wing commentators who think that the government has not gone far enough in taking teacher training out of the hands of HEIs altogether. The establishment of the Teacher Training Agency (TTA) in 1994 was certainly driven by a political imperative to generate an acceptable 'diversity' of routes into teaching. In this period there have been two major developments in teacher education in England and Wales: mentoring and partnerships, and teacher competences.

Mentoring and partnerships

The origins of mentoring in ITE can be traced back over a decade in the UK. In 1987 the Oxford University Department of Educational Studies and its associated schools working with a very supportive LEA introduced the 'internship scheme'. The aim of the programme was clear: 'teachers in school [are] best placed to assist the development of young teachers in training' (Benton, 1990). This development involved collaboration between the school and university in the form of subject teachers becoming mentors and taking a greater part in the training of student teachers, who were placed in pairs, or groups of up to ten, in each school. This move was an early attempt to transfer elements of the responsibility for training teachers to schools. McIntyre (1993) states that students did not learn from the 'educational theorising' they encountered in many teacher education courses. He suggested that they would learn a great deal more in extended school-based experience. Much has been written about this course and the research on it by numerous members of Oxford University's Educational Studies department has had considerable impact on the shape of teacher education. Indeed, there was very much a vanguard quality about the promotion of this particular scheme. The research conducted in Cambridge into mentoring and partnerships (Beardon *et al.*, 1992) found a real lack of clarity in the presentation of the programme, especially in the use of the terms 'school based' and 'partnership'. The researchers found that the task most often delegated to teachers was the assessment of students' practical competence. It was far from clear how the time in school would improve training and HMI (1991) made this very point when they said that 'the quality of training is not a direct product of the amount of time spent in schools'. Nevertheless, there was a growing lobby in favour of greater emphasis being placed on the workplace, which was considered by many as the principal site of professional learning.

The development of partnerships between schools and Higher Education Institutions (HEIs) aimed at the training and education of student teachers long predates the recent arrangements for teacher training. As early as 1982 the DES had commissioned research on such school-based PGCE courses. HMI proposed that partnership between schools and HEIs in the training of teachers should be strengthened. There was clearly an extension of government policy initiatives on teacher education in the 1980s. Circular 3/84 advocated partnerships between schools and HEIs by proposing that experienced teachers be more involved in the preparation of student teachers and also that educational theory be tailored to what the student actually requires to practise teaching in schools. By means of this circular the State intervened, for the first time, to define the content and structure of teacher education. HEIs could no longer simply pass students as suitable for teaching.

The Council for the Accreditation of Teacher Education (CATE) was established to publish the criteria against which courses were to be judged. Before 1984 all HEI-validated courses in Initial Teacher Education automatically led to the status of qualified teacher. In 1988 the Licensed Teacher Scheme was introduced as an alternative route into teaching for mature entrants. This scheme involved two years of training organised by a school teacher mentor according to criteria laid down by the DES. HEIs were not necessarily involved, but LEAs were. In 1989 the Articled Teachers Scheme was introduced, designed as an experiment in school-based training with 80 per cent of time spent in school and 20 per cent in HEI. In this scheme LEAs, schools and the HEI were involved. The criteria for this programme were established by CATE. Successive versions of the CATE criteria became more prescriptive. Both the licensed and articled teachers' training involved supervision by a teacher mentor in school. Circular 24/89 emphasised that mentors were to be prepared for these new roles in teacher education with some training so that they could structure the training of teachers. The circular also required institutions to have a written statement on the role of teachers involved in teacher training.

At the North of England Education Conference in January 1992 the Secretary of State for Education announced another government initiative, a school-based training for all those in initial teacher education. He announced that teacher mentors would be trained and take on real responsibility for the student teachers' learning programme. There was a clear emphasis on partnership. Students would spend 80 per cent of their time in schools and there would be a detailed competency framework. There would be 'joint responsibility' between schools and HEIs and each school would be a 'full partner' and would have a 'leading role'. Resources would be reallocated from HEIs to schools. After he announced these proposals, the Secretary of State said that they would go out for consultation. The circulars did not clarify what was meant by partnership nor show how teachers were to have a 'leading role'.

Whiting *et al.* (1996) have surveyed the partnerships which have so far been formed and have attempted to identify three types or models: collaborative partnerships, HEI-led partnerships and separatist partnerships. They indicate that any individual teacher education course might embody aspects of more than one of these models and they describe each of the models. In the first model, collaborative partnerships have emulated the 'Oxford Internship' model which involves teacher mentors and teacher educators working together in discussing professional issues and planning and delivering the course together. In the second model, HEIs lead partnerships in which they utilise schools as a resource in setting up learning opportunities for students. The HEIs determine the aims, define tasks and what students should learn in schools. There is some consultation over procedural issues, but mentors in schools are 'trained' to deliver what the course defines as necessary. The reason for this type of partnership, Whiting *et al.* suggest, is that some schools may have been unwilling to get involved or to participate in schemes which make demands on teachers and schools. In the third model, HEIs and schools in separatist partnerships are seen as having separate and complementary roles and responsibilities – partnership but not integration in the course. There are no visits from HE tutors in this model and mentor roles are defined with mentoring anchored in the knowledge base of the school. The school would also be responsible for the assessment of student teachers. Whiting *et al.* (1996) have also found that the majority of such partnerships are having great difficulty with the selection of schools, their recruitment to the schemes and the turnover of both schools and mentors.

In a further development, in 1994 the TTA was created by the government to promote diversity in the routes into teaching. Its responsibilities and duties included advice about teacher criteria, allocation of funding, policy development and a concern for quality matters. It replaced CATE and has developed more radical proposals for teacher education. For example, it set up School-Centred Initial Teacher Training (SCITT) schemes which involve consortia of schools taking responsibility for ITE without necessarily involving HEIs as partners. There are a number of such schemes operating and the TTA seems determined to promote them. Less successfully, the government also proposed a one-year, non-graduate training for early years teaching which was directed at parents and others with experience of children. This last proposal represented a major challenge to the idea that teaching involves an expert body of knowledge. The clear implication is that the 'common sense knowledge' of parents is equal to that of the professional teacher. There was overwhelming opposition from the teaching profession to this government-inspired proposal and it was dropped.

OFSTED is responsible for monitoring and for the inspection of teacher education and in order to carry out this responsibility it has retained a small group of HMIs who are directed to make formal assessments of HEIs' compliance with government teacher education criteria. The criteria by which OFSTED makes this assessment of secondary teacher training were published in 1993. It is interesting that OFSTED does not include the participation of schools in ITE schemes as an area of school inspection and yet the TTA proclaims the benefits of such involvement to schools. It seems that the TTA drive to increase school responsibility for teacher education is unlikely to succeed. There is little evidence to suggest that schools want significantly increased responsibilities for teacher education. It is also a matter of concern that TTA consultation is limited and Graham and Barnett (1996) claim that TTA 'consultations have been lengthy bureaucratic exercises in which questionnaires have tightly controlled the agenda'. No real consultation appears to be evident, and this has led, in the main, to the formation of a culture of compliance among teacher educators. The DfE's Circular 14/93 continued government intervention by defining the exact number of hours that should be spent on certain subjects in teacher education and clearly signalled a move to the use of profiles which would contain sets of statements of competence for each student teacher. As with other developments, the central thrust is clear, increasingly directive and centralised moves to impose a model of teacher as 'technician'. The government claims the right to control what teachers teach, how long they will teach for and even the methods that should be used. The announcement in 1996 of the proposed introduction of HEI league tables for teacher education, as well as a national curriculum for teacher education, was, therefore, not surprising.

Teacher competences

An entirely new concept was introduced to ITE in England and Wales in Circular 9/92. The DfE required that, by September 1994, all courses of teacher education must use competence statements in assessing, recording and developing the student teachers' capabilities. Much of the impetus for these radical changes towards a competence-based model in teacher education came from the strategies popularised by the work of the National Council for Vocational Qualifications. The move was also influenced by the industrial skills and training version of competences promoted by the Manpower Services Commission, and both the Training Agency and Further Education Unit. The concept of training, articulated in terms of pre-defined 'outcomes', is not new and even the Council for National Academic Awards had submissions made to it for course validations which included 'competences', although the term 'objectives' was often used or preferred to competences. It is also interesting that mentoring had its origins in the business world.

Behavioural competences are described from task analysis of successful performers. Elliott (1993) has described their basic principle as that of 'behaviourism with its implications that the significance of theoretical knowledge in training is a purely technical or instrumental one'. He also believes that they operate as an 'ideological device for eliminating value issues from the domains of professional practice and thereby subordinating them to political forms of control'. Competency-based teaching is aimed at improving teaching performance in the classroom, so competence is necessarily defined in such a way as to make it measurable. This measurable dimension makes it easy to inspect teachers and teacher educators.

Circular 9/92 contained five general areas of competence: subject knowledge, subject application, class management, assessment and recording of pupils' progress and further professional development. These areas contained a total of twenty-seven more specific competences between them. There is a complete absence of any attempt to define exactly both the 'contexts' and 'levels of proficiency' required of Newly Qualified Teachers' competences. The drive towards the model of teacher-as-technician is again clear, by the use of a central ideological concept of 'competence' which is imported from a business context foreign to the educational world, and imposed without agreement or meaningful consultation.

Hyland (1996) claims that competences have resulted in a reduced teacher education curriculum, a loss of significant theoretical content, restriction of student teacher interaction and the deskilling of work. He suggests that since competences are concerned almost exclusively with 'product' they cannot possibly service the needs of professional studies which are characterised by an emphasis on process, growth and development. It seems, therefore, ironic that the majority of HEIs have supplemented the government's competences list by prescribing a range of their own competences. The widespread use of the government's competences list in teacher education is not surprising considering that HEIs are assessed solely on the government's criteria. Some courses, according to Whiting et al. (1996), however, have been using threshold competences (achieved/not yet achieved) and others have favoured developmental competences (rating different kinds of development).

A REVIEW OF ITE IN SCOTLAND

In order to understand the arrangements for the training of teachers in Scotland, it is first necessary to say something about the country's general educational context. In Scotland there is no National Curriculum or national testing in schools nor are there any equivalents of the TTA, OFSTED or SCAA. Local education authorities are still important partners in educational provision and policy formulation and there are no grant-maintained schools. Scotland has enjoyed a statutory-based General Teaching Council (GTC) for over twenty-five years. This consists of 49 members: 30 from primary, secondary, further and teacher education institutions; 15 from LEAs, universities and the churches and only 4 appointed by the Secretary of State. One of its responsibilities is the review and accreditation of all teacher training programmes and its accreditation committee is composed of practising teachers. Teachers are required by law to be registered with the GTC before they can take up a teaching position in Scotland. There is one dominant teaching union, the Educational Institute of Scotland (EIS), and the HM Inspectorate retains its traditional role within the education system. Teaching has long been a graduate entry profession, at all levels, and there has been no suggestion of diluting this with a 'mums' army'. Critically, there is a more consensual educational climate in Scotland. If we add to this that the Conservative Party remains a small minority party in Scotland and does not control a single local authority, it is within this context that we must understand how the government has attempted to address the two issues of teacher competence and mentoring in Scotland.

A policy on competences

As early as 1989 the Scottish Office Education Department (SOED) and the GTC established working parties to examine teacher education and these committees were broadly representative of the teaching profession. The Department published its *Guidelines for Teacher Training Courses* in 1993 (SOED, 1993a) and was careful to preface it with the comment that they represented a 'revision, updating and consolidation of guidelines' that it had issued since 1983. These *Guidelines*, and they were only guidelines, not directives as with the English and Welsh Circular 9/92, contained the competences for 'beginning teachers'. They were divided into four broad areas relating to: the subject and content of teaching, the classroom, the school and professionalism. The *Guidelines* made it clear that they were not a list of 'can do's' and the tone of the language used implied a low-key approach. Commentators, especially from teacher education, generally welcomed the new competences. Kleinberg (1993) was pleased, 'if not relieved, at the definition of competence as more than performance. The *Guidelines*' definition implies a concept of professional learning and behaviour which recognises the complexity, sophistication and judgement required in teaching.' Brown (1996) felt that the language used in the *Guidelines* implies a subtle stress on professional judgement in contrast to the managerial accountability found in England's teacher competences. Certainly, the

Guidelines emphasised that beginning teachers 'must also display certain professional attitudes – to the job, to pupils, to the school, to parents, to the school board, to the community in general'. The competences were to be seen in terms of understanding and reflection and evaluation.

The fourth broad area of the competences addressed 'professionalism' which related to 'critical thinking' and 'positive attitudes' as well as practical skills. Examples included professional commitments: to the community within and beyond the school; to fairness and equality of opportunity; to the promotion of spiritual and moral education. The annex to the document also refers to courses demonstrating how theory relates to practice. The teacher competences in Scotland were the product of consultation and they emphasise professional values and leave it to the teacher institutions to devise their own competences based on the Scottish Office's *Guidelines*. There were, however, a number of criticisms from both the teacher unions and researchers. Brown (1996) describes how the convenor of the Educational Institute of Scotland looked at the competences and asked whether Scotland needs teachers who are 'semi-skilled technicians' or 'professionals who in addition to teaching effectively remain active thinkers'. Carr (1993a) has been extremely critical of the competences found in the *Guidelines* and points to what they have become in England. He believes that they are inadequate for dealing with the complexities of professional expertise and feels that no good reason has been offered to support the assumption that increased school experience would, of itself, improve the overall quality of teaching in schools. Nevertheless, the competences in Scotland, in contrast to those in England, give more emphasis to the development of professional values and judgement.

However, there were many others who criticised the competency-based account of SOED-required skills and attitudes for teachers. Stromach *et al.* (1994) detail how the competences were seen by many as a threat to the autonomy of the profession and point out that the debate in the Scottish education press was anti-competences. The idea that the government should determine what teachers should teach and how they should teach it did not receive support from the teaching profession. Stromach *et al.* (1994) believed that the *Guidelines* could be seen as constituting a national curriculum for teaching and that they gave the State the mechanism with which to generate tighter control of teacher education. The debate was certainly over-polarised. However, Stromach *et al.* (1994) also felt that the use of adjectives like 'suitable' and 'appropriate' softened the competences compared to those in England and Wales. Their research indicated that the *Guidelines* offered a hopelessly over-extended view of professional achievement in relation to the 'beginning teacher'. They found that the beginning teacher experienced more incompetence than competence and that the SOED competences had an idealistic and remote air to them.

Mentoring

The second mechanism which the SOED attempted to introduce into the Scottish education system was mentoring. In May 1994 the SOED issued a press release which informed schools and teacher institutions that a mentoring scheme would be introduced in August 1995 and would include a role for classroom teachers to participate in the 'supervision, training and assessment of students' preparing for teaching. The SOED had conducted a pilot study of mentoring the previous year but it was not at all clear what mentoring meant in the context of Scottish education. Much of the literature used in support of the case for mentoring emanated from south of the border, especially from the Oxford Internship Scheme. Research in Scotland had shown that teachers supported teacher education remaining within higher education and that they supported theoretically informed student teachers (Stark, 1994). Nevertheless, the SOED pursued its own directive, which included an increase of school-based experience at PGCE level from 50 per cent to 58 per cent. Money was eventually made available to train new mentors, who were to be allocated 80 minutes of 'protected time' per student per week. Mentor training materials would be provided from the SOED and there would be selection criteria for mentors. The Secretary of the SOED at a Department Seminar on Partnership in Initial Teacher Training held in November 1993 (SOED, 1993b), which was designed to consult on mentoring, commented that 'There was still no clear and simple consensus on what was best done in school and what was best done in college'. There was no mention of schools 'taking the lead' in partnership with the teacher education institutions and there was a clear avoidance of control by schools of teacher education. The teacher education institutions were still to have control of teacher education. It was announced at this seminar that there would be no new money and that the changes to teacher education would have to come from existing funds. Within two weeks the SOED was forced to change its view on this and additional money was provided for its proposed partnership scheme.

Nevertheless, the EIS, at its annual conference, voiced early concerns about the mentoring scheme, in particular the expected workload on teachers who would be responsible for implementing the scheme. It also did not feel that the government would continue to resource it once it had been established as practice in schools. Interestingly, the Institute also felt that the professionalism of teachers would suffer by student teachers spending longer periods in school and less time in college (*The Scotsman*, 22 July 1995). Teacher educators, who were also members of the EIS, were concerned at the speed at which the changes in 'training' were being introduced. Local authorities also objected to the mentoring scheme because of the likely impact on pupils' learning and they were worried about the reaction of parents. The government's response was to send letters to all headteachers in Scottish schools seeking their support for the scheme and it even produced a video to persuade parents of the benefits of mentoring. In July 1995 the government, after failing to secure support for the scheme from any of these groups, announced a one-year delay in implementing mentoring in schools. By October the Scottish education minister had been moved and the government announced that the scheme had been dropped.

The government then invited the GTC to establish a working party to look at new ways of developing partnership between schools and the teacher institutions. The government asked the Council to report back to it in six months. The Council accepted the invitation, but said it would not be in a position to report back to the SOED until it had something to report. Teacher education in Scotland has returned to its pre-1994 position, which includes 50 per cent of time in college. There are no mentors in schools, which means that compared to England there has been substantially less change in the education of teachers in Scotland. The ability to resist government policy on mentoring, which many believed had been imported from right-wing groups in England, was largely due to the existence of a GTC and the strong consensus culture in Scottish education. As Tomlinson (1995b) says: 'As usual, the Scots are taking a more thoughtful ... approach.' The apparent immunity of Scotland from the worst excesses of policy on ITE is perhaps due to the general hostility the Scots have displayed towards the ideologically driven policies of central government since 1979. Teachers and HEIs in England and Wales might perhaps profit from a study of the factors which enabled Scottish ITE to offer successful resistance.

A REVIEW OF ITE IN NORTHERN IRELAND

Arrangements for initial teacher education were reviewed in response to the consultation paper *Teachers for the 21st Century: A Review of Initial Teacher Training* (Department of Education Northern Ireland (DENI), 1991). DfE Circular 9/92 furthered that review process when three working groups were established. The three working groups produced reports on: Competences; Courses, Cooperation and ITT Structures; Coordination of ITT, Induction and In-service Training (DENI, 1993a). Following the reports of the three working groups, a fourth group, the Development Group, was established to consider as a whole the implications for ITT. Subsequently, the Development Group recommended 'that teacher education in Northern Ireland should take place in three coordinated Stages: Stage I: Initial Teacher Training; Stage II: Induction; Stage III: The Further Professional Development of Teachers' (DENI, 1993b: 3). After the period of initial teacher education, 'provisionally qualified teachers' would follow a two-year period of support and induction, satisfactory completion of which 'should lead to qualified teacher status' (DENI, 1993a: 22–23). NQTs would then move into the period of Further Professional Development. Each stage would be supported by the most appropriate member of the HEI–school partnerships.

An action plan for implementation was developed: 1993–1994 was to be the preparatory year; in 1994–1995 the first secondary courses under the new arrangements were to begin; while in 1996–1997, all secondary courses were to be school-based. A similar programme for development of primary courses was also proposed (DENI, 1993b: 11–13). Other proposals included the establishment of a Coordinating Committee for Teacher Education in Northern Ireland, which the group hoped might evolve into a General Teaching Council for Northern Ireland – even though the group recognised 'that such a matter was not within the terms of reference of Group IV' (DENI, 1993b: 8–10).

Competences and professional values

The report of Working Group I on competences (DENI, 1993a) is possibly the most significantly different approach to the development of a competence-based model of teacher education described thus far: first, because of its insistence on the need to view competences as 'developmental' rather than 'minimum thresholds' (par. 18) and, second, for the group's acknowledgement of the 'Professional Characteristics of the Successful Teacher' (par. 15) which underpin and unify the development of competence.

The clearest example of the group's thinking with respect to the developmental nature of competences is to be found in its proposals in relation to three co-ordinated stages of teacher education: Stage I: Initial Teacher Training; Stage II: Induction; Stage III: The Further Professional Development of Teachers (DENI, 1993a: 6–15). In drawing up the list of competences, the group related them to each of the three stages of teacher education, acknowledging that development of competence goes far beyond the period of initial teacher education. Furthermore, the group 'weighted' the competences by indicating which competences were most likely to be developed during which stage: for example, the development of an 'understanding of the arguments in favour of a balanced and broadly based curriculum' is appropriate to Stage I and may be achieved with little or no school experience; whereas 'takes appropriate responsibility for curriculum leadership' is more likely to be appropriate to Stages II or III. A full list of the Northern Ireland competences may be found in Appendix A.

Competence and context

The arguments central to the debate about competence-based models and assessment of teacher education are rehearsed in Chapter 2, but it is worth noting here Working Group I's thinking, which led to the development of the Northern Ireland model of competence-based teacher education. The group's central point lies in the belief that lists of simple, behavioural competences are at best mechanistic and take 'little account of the fact that in real life a competence can only be applied in specific contexts' (par. 6). Given the variety of provision in schooling in Northern Ireland in selective/non-selective schools, many of which are small and in rural areas, it is unsurprising that a debate about the context of the demonstration of competence should surface.

In the following paragraph the development of professional competence is discussed in relation to the central unifying part played by knowledge, understandings and attitudes and the need to view them as permeating and affecting practice in very specific and particular performances. Little is gained by possession of a competence if one cannot judge when to use it. One advantage of applying this perspective to teaching is that it can accommodate the strong dimension of values which is present in professional activities of this nature.

(par. 7)

Like the Scottish Office Education Department (SOED), the working group took the view that 'professional competences' should be understood as referring 'to knowledge, understanding and attitudes as well as to practical skills' (par. 11). Such an approach, the group believed, could provide 'the basis for elaborating a fully developed concept of a reflective practitioner' (par. 7). Although assessment becomes more complex in such a model of competence, it does mean that the 'professional judgement of teachers and teacher educators' (par. 7) is recognised and valued.

Professional values

The atomisation of professional knowledge, judgement and skill into discrete competences inevitably fails to capture the essence of professional competence.

(DENI, 1993a: 4)

In order to respond to the call for the development of competence-based teacher education courses and to overcome the deficiencies in reductive lists of competences, Working Group I identified the 'personal qualities' and 'professional attitudes' which enable the teacher to unify and synthesise knowledge, understandings and experience gained in the professional context and 'to pull the individual competences together and apply them in the professional context' (DENI, 1993a: 4). Professional characteristics are at the core of the teacher's development of professional knowledge and professional skills. The group's 'Professional Characteristics of the Successful Teacher' may be found in Appendix B.

The 'values' dimension of teaching is fully debated in Chapter 3, but it is worth noting here that it is only the Northern Ireland model of competence which includes a discussion of this dimension in any depth. The working group was aware that such characteristics are 'general (and perhaps ideal)', but acknowledging that teaching dwells in the realms of the ideal, strengthens the model. Working Group I acknowledges also that these permeating characteristics are not fixed, but are, like the other competences, developmental in their nature: 'In describing characteristics in this way we are not, of course, suggesting that they are innate, and that "good teachers are born and not made": these qualities too can be fostered and developed' (DENI, 1993a: 4).

Teachers need to develop knowledge and understanding of the content and processes of teaching and learning a National Curriculum subject as well as craft skills of classroom management, and they also need to develop the ability to evaluate and justify their actions. Furthermore, the group believed that teachers 'also need an appreciation of the broader context in which they are working' (par. 11). Clearly, the need for this dimension in relation to 'the particular concerns in Northern Ireland for education for mutual understanding and cultural heritage' (DENI, 1993b: 2) can be appreciated. However, it is this wider perspective and the 'values' dimension which are absent from most other competence-based models: an absence which, therefore, diminishes them.

Mentoring

The reports of all groups make it clear that any move towards a school-based model of teacher education and professional development would need to be supported by a thorough programme of planned mentor training. Working Group II developed a wide definition of the mentor:

> Traditional concepts of mentoring appear to suppose that all mentors are school teachers relating to their own school and that courses can be provided to train them. The Group proposes that this is not necessarily true in an as yet unexplored mass system of school-based training and there will be need for flexibility and the capacity for development. Consequently, the Group has adopted the model of a mentor who is a teacher or tutor, school or institution based; a person with a new or developed role arising from school-based training.
>
> (DENI, 1993a: 25)

The processes of mentoring are discussed in detail in Chapters 5, 6 and 7, but it is interesting to note that, within approximately five years, accepted mentoring practices which grew out of the Oxford University Internship Scheme have come to be regarded as 'traditional' by educationalists. The Development Group widened the definition of mentor further to include Education Library Board (ELB) support staff and proposed that a scheme of general mentor training be developed by the Coordinating Committee for Teacher Education in consultation with HEIs, schools and ELBs (DENI, 1993b: 12). Working Group III briefly outlined the purposes of such mentor training:

> Such a scheme of training, perhaps in modular form, must pre-pare mentors for their counselling, professional, curriculum and management roles as required. The training in the curriculum and professional roles will be based largely upon developing the competences of the teacher.
>
> (DENI, 1993a: 34)

The Group went a step further by proposing the establishment of a 'Clearing House' to which schools would apply to join school-based partnerships. The Clearing House would then 'be responsible for confirming that a school meets the criteria for designation as a training school' (DENI, 1993b: 35–36). Yet again the process of discussion and consultation in Northern Ireland yielded a more sophisticated proposed model than the one in England and Wales. While acknowledging that the size of the Province, with fewer schools and HEIs engaged in the preparation of teachers, makes such a proposal more manageable, there is evidence of a more considered, holistic approach to the development of initial teacher education than in England and Wales, which has been characterised by dictate on the basis of little or no consultation of the parties involved. Rather, the driving force in recent years appears to have come from writers associated with the New Right, such as O'Hear (1988), the Hillgate Group (1989) and Lawlor (1990), whose task has been: 'To reproduce the pure ideology of Thatcherism in the particular context of initial training, to reconstruct and re-present the preparation of teachers in accordance with the ideological principles of the government' (Wilkin, 1996: 166).

Innovation and evolution

The proposed changes to the Northern Ireland model were radical and far-reaching. The process of discussion and consultation continued until the spring of 1996, by which time it had become apparent that there were clear divisions among the various parties who would be involved in school-based teacher education: HEIs, schools, Education Library Boards (ELBs) and the Governing Bodies Association (GBA), among others. Without doubt, the context of schooling in Northern Ireland influenced the outcomes. Working Group IV had acknowledged that any developments would need to have regard to

> The structure of Secondary schools in Northern Ireland; the high proportion of small schools, especially small rural Primary schools in Northern Ireland; and, the particular concerns in Northern Ireland for education for mutual understanding and cultural heritage.
>
> (DENI, 1993b: 2)

Resistance to the new model came from some of the grammar schools, a number of which showed initial interest in developing their own SCITT schemes. Furthermore, many perceived the changes as unnecessary. Such an attitude is, perhaps, understandable in the light of the high-quality graduates recruited to PGCE secondary courses, for example. Competition for the limited number of places on such courses is strong. Approximately 45 per cent of Northern Ireland's graduates have to leave the Province in order to pursue postgraduate studies. Similarly, incentives for change were seen as poor. In order to have regard to Circular 9/92, the Development Group discussed the transfer funds from HEIs to partnership schools. However, the government's hope that such sums should recognise 'the increased contribution of partner schools to teacher training' (DfE, 1992: 4) was in many cases forlorn. The sums on offer were seen as derisory. Coupled to the general sense of innovation overload that many teachers felt, there was a general reluctance on the part of teachers to take on more responsibility for the development and assessment of student teachers in a partnership model. It should be noted, however, that schools were prepared to continue to engage in teacher education along 'traditional' lines, and, indeed, that in many cases, teachers were actually engaging in what would be characterised as 'mentoring' in such schemes.

Subsequently, in April 1996, the Minister for Education in Northern Ireland stated that the development of partnerships should be 'evolutionary'. 'It will continue to be for each school to decide whether and to what extent it wishes to participate in providing teacher education placements' (DENI, 1996: 3). After the almost perpetual change and innovation in education in the early 1990s, it is unsurprising that, when offered the choice of taking on one further innovation, many teachers and schools declined the offer. For the foreseeable future, schools, ELBs and HEIs would build upon established good practice at a pace that best suited the needs and interests of those engaged in teacher education. While such a compromise is understandable, and perhaps laudable, the corollary is that there is a risk, therefore, that quality of provision for teacher education in Northern Ireland will become more, not less, varied. Part of the intention of developing competence-based programmes was the perceived need of 'output measures' which would help to do away with the marked variability of experience offered to student teachers and which might help to guarantee consistency of quality across institutions, teachers, lecturers and mentors involved in ITT schemes (DENI, 1993a: 1).

CONCLUSION

This chapter has shown that the extent to which mentoring and competence-led models of ITE have been introduced in England, Scotland and Northern Ireland has varied in relation to the different political processes whereby educational change is brought about in those parts of the United Kingdom. It is also a relatively new phenomenon, one which is still no more than ten years old. As such, it is still early to say exactly what has happened, let alone what the detailed consequences may be. Nevertheless, a number of provisional observations can be made in conclusion to this chapter which might help subject mentors to consider further some of the issues which have been raised.

Subject mentors might wish to ask themselves what model of the teacher is at the heart of their partnership scheme. There are clearly a number of different claims about the type of models of teacher education being operated by various partnership schemes, ranging from reflective practitioner models to competence-led models. Mentors should be able to compare the claims made for the partnership to which they contribute with both their experience of its operation in practice, and their vision of what the most worthwhile form of partnership would look like. Subject mentors will also recognise that 'partnerships' are only genuine when they themselves are fully involved in them, which has implications for the amount of time subject mentors are given for mentoring.

In addition, it should also be realised that there is a 'compliance culture', perhaps through necessity, developing among teachers and teacher educators in regard to teacher education. The government's requirements for teacher education must be complied with if institutions are to continue in the education of teachers. *The Draft Framework for the Assessment of the Quality and Standards in Initial Teacher Training*, issued by OFSTED and the TTA in September 1996, makes it absolutely clear that institutions will be inspected against criteria which above all determine whether or not they meet the requirements of the relevant government circulars. Institutions or schools which fail to meet these government requirements face the threat of withdrawal of funding. In this situation it is not surprising that teacher educators are almost entirely compliant with government policy on teacher education. Despite HEI insistence on reflective models of teacher education, the evidence points clearly to a competence model of teacher education emerging. Indeed, against the rhetoric of 'reflection' most HEIs have instituted detailed competences supplementary to those introduced by the government and the overwhelming majority have officially complied with government policy on inspection.

Further, there has been a real lack of government dialogue with teacher educators, including subject mentors in schools. The argument in this chapter, and in subsequent chapters, is that the introduction of competency-led teacher education has the potential to reduce teachers to little more than 'technicians' and this has deprofessionalised both teachers and teacher educators. Resistance to government policy has been minimal in England and Wales and therefore contrasts sharply with the response of the teaching profession in Scotland. In Northern Ireland there has been greater dialogue than in England and Wales, which has led to a more sophisticated and some would say realistic view of the professional development and education of teachers. The situation is thus stark in England and Wales as partnership schemes are under threat of continuing inspection against harder-edged criteria designed to move partnerships towards more exacting teacher competences. This raises a potential threat to the teaching profession as a whole since the idea of the teacher-as-technician, 'delivering' a pre-packaged National Curriculum, does not sit well with the status of a profession.

2

THE LIMITATIONS OF ASSESSMENT

Now this is what some great men are very slow to allow; they insist that Education should be confined to some particular and narrow end, and should issue in some definite work, which can be weighed and measured. They argue as if everything, as well as every person, had its price; and that where there has been great outlay, they have a right to expect a return in kind.

(John Henry Newman: *The Idea of a University*)

INTRODUCTION

Assessment of teachers, both in ITE and in-service, has for some years been the subject of intense political scrutiny and increasingly hostile political comment. Successive Secretaries of State for Education have called for the sacking of 'incompetent' teachers. HM Chief Inspector has stated that student teachers who perform badly should be 'chucked out' of the profession at a much earlier stage than at present (*TES*, 21 June 1996: 8). Indeed a cross-party consensus has emerged, with the Shadow Secretary of State echoing demands for 'bad teachers' to be sacked. In autumn 1996 Michael Barber (1996), a leading adviser to the Labour Party, published *The Learning Game: Arguments for an Education Revolution*, advocating five-yearly examinations for teachers in post, who would be dismissed if they failed. A consensus appears to have been reached which views teachers as technicians who are to be judged against criteria of 'production', and summarily removed if these are not met.

It is instructive to compare this stance with the 'official' view. OFSTED (1995) found the overwhelming majority of teacher training courses 'satisfactory or better'. The Annual Report of the HM Chief Inspector for 1994/95 noted that teacher training 'courses

28

have been carefully planned to comply with the criteria in Circular 9/92'. HEIs, in other words, have carefully followed government policy, and yet they are still subject to continuous criticism. Nevertheless, distrustful of their own inspections, OFSTED and the TTA have introduced tougher standards in the inspection criteria for teacher training and in November 1996 began a second sweep of ITE institutions, only four months after their last inspection. The Secretary of State has declared that HEIs are also to be subject to performance tables (*TES*, 24 May 1996: 1). In addition, HEIs were told to prepare for a 50 per cent increase in ITE places by 2001. This increase has suddenly been dramatically reduced to 3 per cent because the government has announced changes to the procedures by which teachers may retire. These changes will have the effect of retaining many teachers within the profession who wished to take early retirement. Elsewhere, in a DfEE press release, the Secretary of State (192/96, 12 June 1996) has warned of a 'radical agenda' for the reform of teacher training. 'For the first time,' she states, 'we will define the essential content of training courses' (a National Curriculum for teacher training). In-service courses are to be recast in terms of competences; teacher appraisal will be used to 'correct weaknesses' in staff development. All this is 'just a start'. In September 1996 the Secretary of State announced the introduction of a defined National Teacher Training Curriculum to cover: knowledge of subject; what pupils should be taught; effective teaching and assessment methods; and standards of achievement expected of pupils. The TTA (TTA Circular 27/96) has been asked to introduce these measures 'urgently', beginning with English and Mathematics for primary teacher training in 1997 and Science to follow in 1998. Secondary teacher education will also have a National Curriculum introduced in all three of these subject areas in September 1998.

And what has been the corollary of such high-profile action? The University Council for the Education of Teachers (UCET) found that the drop-out rate for teacher training courses has risen by 40 per cent (10 per cent to 14 per cent). Recruitment to PGCE courses is falling short of target, intimating critical future teacher shortages in many subject areas. It has apparently not occurred to the DfEE that the constant barrage of abuse directed at teachers has any effect on recruitment rates (see Hillman, 1994). The furore about 'bad teachers' does of course have the advantage of diverting attention from questions of pay and resources in schools. Resources are particularly important since many undergraduates consider that the poor physical fabric of many schools, according to Hillman's (1994) research, provides the teaching profession with an extremely poor working environment – for many an extremely important criterion for choosing a career.

ASSESSMENT AND THE EDUCATION SYSTEM

As has been stated above, assessments have become a central feature of educational practice, and seem likely to remain so for the fore-seeable future. These assessments are supposed to be judgements about the quality, value, effectiveness or impact of educational proce-dures and learning. The assumption behind these assessments seems to be that only that which can be judged quantitatively should be used as the basis for assessment. The assessment is therefore consid-ered unproblematic and relatively easy to carry out. The more complex areas within teaching and learning, such as values and a person's attitude, range and development, are left out. Questions concerning 'context', 'resources', 'bias', 'validity', 'reliability', 'fair-ness', 'effectiveness', 'objectivity', and much more besides, are simply not addressed, or at least are assumed to be no cause for concern. Tomlinson (1995a) discusses the relevance of each of these areas in the assessment of student teachers, particularly the difference that the teaching context, pupils and resources can make to any assess-ment process. It is clear for whom the assessments are intended, since, with the introduction of league tables and school inspection reports, the government believes that parents require this informa-tion to make choices. Schools therefore publish raw data that indicate to parents that we have 'effective' schools with 'competent' teachers and less 'effective' schools with less 'competent' teachers. However, nowhere is it suggested in these tables that teaching is an intensely value-laden, multifaceted and context-specific activity that can never be assessed fully. In-service teachers, as Tickle (1992) says, are increas-ingly being subjected to government-led 'dismissal-driven, manager-ialist monitoring appraisal' and DfE guidelines on student teachers are increasingly phrased in 'deficiency-oriented' and 'selecting-out' tones. Tickle also points out that there are gaping inadequacies con-cerning the assessment of practical teaching in DfE documentation.

Nevertheless, assessment is essential to the educational enterprise, for we need to assure ourselves that we are preparing NQTs who are effective teachers. Therefore, assessment methods used in education need to be carefully planned. There has been a growing distrust of normative assessment procedures, especially in regard to vocational and professional qualifications. The assessment of student teachers has in the past been conducted solely within the internal conventions of an HEI that have not generally been made public. Sometimes these procedures have been no more than loose guidelines for judging teaching quality and have focused on how one student might compare with another, rather than on whether or not the student teacher has met the criteria required to do the job. The DfE's teacher competence statements attempt to increase accountability and consistency of assessment through the detailed articulation of course aims. Student teachers are to be clear about what is expected from them. However, because of the complexity of teaching, it is not always possible to say immediately that a particular lesson went well or not. Indeed, it is the argument of this book that teaching is not reducible to a set of technical operations even when assessment is largely confined to demonstrating classroom competence.

It is now quite common for a student teacher's final assessment to be constructed from formative evidence that is then used for a summative document which informs us where a student is at a certain point in the course (see Stephens, 1996). Formative assessments provide the information which mentors need to identify and describe student teachers' achievements and development priorities. They are, therefore, very much concerned with growth. Summative assessments are judgemental statements and we need to be clear about what it is that is being judged. In order to ascertain this, it is necessary to turn to the concept of 'competence' in teachers, and the question of how far 'competence' is measurable in terms of 'competences'.

COMPETENCES AND ASSESSMENT

As discussed in Chapter 1, competence-based approaches to teacher education have been met with considerable suspicion. One reason is that competence is tied to assessment, usually summative assessment, and that ITE is a compulsory period of training which is formally assessed. The government's list of teacher competences purports to be value- and context-free and yet they are clearly not free-standing assessment instruments, for they always need reference to context and purpose. Nevertheless, a range of assessment methods can be employed even with the use of teacher competences. It is important, therefore, for mentors to recognise exactly what it is they are assessing and at what stage of development. There can be only a limited number of competence areas that beginning teachers can be expected to master in one year of experience in a school. This begs the question of whether there is indeed a definitive list of free-standing competences required from a student teacher and, if so, what these competences are. Are they mental or physical character-istics of a person? Are they pieces of behaviour or action, or even an overall product?

Context, too, is often neglected in the use of teacher competences (see Norris, 1991). Competences also generally give no indication of the level of proficiency a student teacher has reached. Some (cited in Ashworth and Saxton, 1990) have claimed that the notion of teacher competences provides an objective approach to assessment and that it will give new credibility to qualifications such as the PGCE. The TTA has accepted this argument uncritically. However, it is our view that competences are not as reliable or as valid an objec-tive, transferable assessment scheme as some would like to believe, for in their use there is an unavoidable element of subjectivity. As Ashworth and Saxton (1990) say, the assessment of competences 'is superficially attractive since it appears to guarantee a certain level of ability which may be expected to be transferable from the specific sit-uation in which it was acquired'. Tomlinson (1995b) says that many have confused the issue of teacher competences and he takes a more moderate line than either Elliott (1993) or Hyland (1993). He believes that the DfE's teacher competences can be used since the gov-ernment has given some freedom in their implementation. He believes that clarity of purpose in teacher education does not necessarily mean or imply the adoption of a behaviourist training approach. He nev-ertheless rejects a view of teacher competence as prescribed behaviour practice. Whitty (1992) also believes that outright rejection of teacher competence statements may be too hasty a move, for he feels that it is important to recognise that they can be more flexible and adapt-able than at first sight appears.

The context of assessment is particularly important and this has been recognised by the NCVQ (1989: 4), in whose criteria and pro-cedures it is stated that 'the area of competence to be covered must have meaning and relevance in the context of the occupational struc-ture in the sector of employment concerned'. Tomlinson (1995a) believes that teacher competences should be used developmentally. Such use encourages a developmental baseline approach to assessment, which means that whilst the student may be 'satisfactory' for a par-ticular stage of a course, in end-of-course terms he or she may need to improve somewhat. In other words, competences may be used in formative assessment. Such an approach implies that mentors would need to have a clear notion of appropriate end-of-course levels of proficiency. Implicit in the question 'Is the student capable of reaching a certain level of competence?' is the notion of different stages of teacher competence, and research by Stromach *et al.* (1994) may give us some indication of the direction in which we should go.

Teacher competences do not apply universally in all settings and contexts and in Tomlinson's view teacher competences should be used only as a focus. Competences are usually demonstrable or at least observable. If they cannot be observed then it is impossible to assess them or report on them objectively. Tomlinson (1995a) advocates a change of language in the use of teacher competence statements. He speaks of 'intelligent achievement capacity', which is not about single acts of teaching or merely what has been 'covered' in the course, but rather about what a person can do with intelligence. Assessment, he argues, is a matter of gaining evidence of this intelligence, and, he concludes:

> If competences are relatively consistent capacities to achieve particular types of purpose in particular sorts of context, then valid assessment must be based on evidence of relatively consistent achievement of such purposes in such contexts. The further the evidence from such achievements and contexts, the more doubt as to its validity.

Tomlinson (1995a) provides details of how this type of assessment procedure works in practice by describing the arrangements used by the University of Leeds in its partnership with schools. These incorporate statements of levels of proficiency in teaching and employ open-ended report boxes in order to stress the value-laden nature of teaching. Husbands (1993) would no doubt agree with many of these procedures for assessment, but he points out that the aggregating of separately assessed competence components does not necessarily add up to an assessment of the whole. Hyland (1993: 130) goes even further and says:

> Programmes based on the functional analysis of work roles are likely to produce teachers who are 'competent' yet ill-equipped for further professional development, uncritical of educational change and largely ignorant of the wider cultural, social and political context in which the role of teachers needs to be located.

However, Tomlinson stresses the value commitment aspects of teaching and emphasises that in using the government's teacher competences pluralism of practice should prevail, especially in terms of the use of broad assessment methods which promote a student teacher's development. Teaching, he says, is not achievable through any single set of procedures for it demands flexible application from a complex repertoire built up over many years of teaching experience. He concludes his discussion of competences and assessment by making it clear that teacher competence specifications have the potential, and only the potential, to be reference frameworks for three overlapping functions: *assessment*, both formative and summative; *development*, which encourages reflection, understanding and growth; and *communication and reflection*, which involve both student teacher and mentor. Tomlinson's proposed use of the teacher competences appears both reasonable and practicable enough to be used by mentors for assessment purposes.

Clearly then there appears to be some scope for partnerships between HEIs and schools to develop their own distinct approaches to assessing teacher competences. As Furlong (1995) notes: 'the Circular (9/92) is open to narrow as well as broad interpretations. A narrowly mechanistic approach to initial teacher education is not demanded by the Circular. If that is the result it will be because we have imposed it on ourselves.' But, with OFSTED inspections of ITE focusing primarily on whether DfE competences are being used, coupled with the TTA's development of competence-based Career Entry Profiles, the scope for 'broad interpretations' is being progressively limited. In any case, research (Whiting *et al.*, 1996) indicates that the majority of ITE partnerships use the DfE competences extensively in assessment. What are then the official requirements for assessment?

ASSESSMENT REQUIREMENTS

Conditions for the award of Qualified Teacher Status (Annex A, par. 3.4.1) are framed by the DfE simply as demonstrating in the classroom:

- the ability to teach effectively and to secure effective learning;
- the ability to manage pupil behaviour.

The DfE declares that 'The progressive development of these competences should be monitored regularly during initial training', and

'Their attainment at a level appropriate to NQT should be the objective of every student taking a course of training' (Annex A, par. 2.1). Clearly, competences are to be used in assessing, recording and developing student teachers' teaching capabilities. The circular does not define the actual nature of the competence that beginning teachers should have nor how they should be monitored and so par. 11 states: 'It is recognised that institutions are developing their own competence-based approaches to the assessment of students.' No formal assessment approach is recommended in this circular, although in the government's *Proposals for the Reform of ITT* (1993) there is a clear move to the use of profiles containing sets of teacher competence statements. The TTA (1996b) is already developing Career Entry Profiles, although these are not to be introduced until 1998, and is also actively producing professional national standards for four points in a teacher's career, coupled with qualifications. These points or stages are described as end of training, subject leader, expert teacher and headteacher.

There is considerable variation in the way ITE partnerships fulfil the assessment requirements of the DfE. The growing literature on ITE partnership arrangements gives detailed descriptive accounts of particular secondary PGCE courses, including: Oxford (Benton, 1990), Cambridge (Beardon et al., 1992), Leicester (Everton and White, 1992), Manchester (Reid, 1994), Warwick (Robinson, 1994), Newcastle (Field, 1994), East Anglia (Husbands, 1994), Leeds (Tomlinson, 1995a), York (Stephens, 1996) and the Open University (Moon and Shelton Mayes, 1995). There are common elements to be found in the course documentation in these ITE partnerships which include: the use of competences in both formative and summative assessments; student folders or portfolios containing all the accessible products of the course; and a series of specific points on the courses at which judgements are made about a student teacher's progress. 'Reflective self development' and 'reflective practice' (discussed in Chapter 4) are also stated as being prominent in the majority of these courses. Course written assignments are designed to encourage student teachers to take full account of the relationship between a mature, critical understanding of the subject specialism and the acquisition of competences. Assessment in all of the courses appears to be progressive and continuous, in the sense that the student teacher builds up evidence for the achievement of the competences over the course as a whole. Some of these schemes, such as the Open University partnership, seek to integrate professional values into teacher education and emphasise a developmental approach to the competence statements, which gives the student teacher the responsibility to present evidence of achievement. Recognising failure, or cause for concern, in student teachers at any particular stage in the course is not easy and whilst most partnership course documentation is good on procedures for dealing with such students, it is not so good on articulating guidance on recognising them. It is usually a matter left to the professional judgement of mentors and HEI tutors. The question of how a student teacher's teaching performance, identified in competences, relates to overall teacher competence is also not really explained in most of these schemes. Similarly, consideration of quality assurance in mentors' use of assessment techniques raises further issues about the need for consistency of assessment procedures. It is therefore advisable to examine the relationship between the mentor and assessment.

MENTORING AND ASSESSMENT

One of the tasks of mentors is the assessment of student teachers' competences in the subject classroom and in the school. It is mentors who are largely responsible for the difficult decisions about the progress of student teachers. However, not all mentors are equipped to assess, for as OFSTED (1995) reported: 'few mentors are yet confident in the assessment of students' performance'. Research by Elliott and Calderhead (1993) also found that mentors in the Articled Teacher Scheme were sometimes uncomfortable about challenging teachers over needed improvement. Mentors certainly monitor the students' progress by watching them, providing advice and constructive criticism. In addition, the mentor's judgement about a particular student can be validated by other mentors in the school and external tutors and examiners.

Essentially, there are two methods of assessment in teacher education: first, where the school assesses on its own criteria; second, where the school, in collaboration with an HEI, designs a set of common criteria. In the second method there is concurrence, or agreement, between schools and HEIs about the skills new teachers are expected to manifest in their teaching practice. Mentors within partnership schemes are, therefore, not alone in making these difficult decisions. Nevertheless, there are certain pitfalls in assessing students. There is always a danger that mentors could damage students with unfounded personally based judgements. Wilkin (1992) says that mentor 'hunches' are unquantifiable and should not be the basis of assessment in ITE. It is also the case that mentor judgements of students can be skewed in favour of their own view of the student, which can lead to a personality clash or the 'halo effect' – a student shining or failing in the mentor's own particular area of interest. These two common pitfalls need to be recognised and mentors should ensure that they are familiar with the assessment regulations in the documentation of their partnership courses (see Dart and Drake, 1996).

Nevertheless, intuitive inferences or tacit insights by mentors are inevitable, especially since informal observation of student teachers occurs far more frequently than formal assessments and therefore can be the most influential type of data in assessing student teachers. Holmes (1992) describes how a number of performance indicators were identified in the Northamptonshire Licensed Teacher Scheme which included: the general appearance of the student; facial impression (whether the student smiled); illness, absence, fewer referrals of pupils; out-of-class activities; whether the pupils enjoyed the lessons given by the student; and many more besides. These types of performance indicators, whilst not often specified, are also used in PGCE courses, but they are subjective and informal assessments which are being made by the mentor throughout the school experience and some are also context-bound in that they are specific, or particular, to a certain school. The assessment of such performance indicators is often more difficult than their recognition. There is also the question of parity across schools and different mentors which is difficult to achieve.

Hagger *et al.* (1993) have suggested that post-lesson debriefings should consist of data collected during the mentor's observations and only described to the student, if necessary, but not evaluated by the mentor. The onus is on giving the student objective non-judgemental feedback so as to encourage the student to give an explanation of what the mentor has observed. This leads to student teachers evaluating their own performance and talking through their reason-ing with the mentor. Obviously this method of debriefing is designed to assist student teachers in their reflection on teaching. It combines competences with the notion of the 'reflective practitioner'. Consequently, mentors listen to student teachers, ask open questions and write down what is said for reference. Assessment of this kind is both on-going and implicit in mentoring acts, but there can be tension when the mentor moves from support to judgement. Therefore, while mentors recognise the needs of student teachers and highlight their successes, there is also a need to inform student teachers about any formative assessment that has been recorded, so that they are always encouraged to reflect and self-evaluate. Target setting in particular can help in this process.

Targets are often short-term priorities resulting from formative assessments. These targets must be articulated precisely, preferably given to the student in writing and be few in number. There should follow a formal review of student teacher progress after a specified and agreed time has elapsed. Targets are either fulfilled by the student or need to be revised with the mentor. Failure to meet the targets should result in both student and mentor isolating the causes. As Jaworski and Watson (1994) note, the mentor must be able to be critical even when criticism is unwelcome. However, the mentor might usefully keep in mind such questions as:

- Is my assessment of the student teacher accurate – have I sufficient evidence for my opinion?
- Is my assessment of the student fair – or is my judgement being clouded by personal preferences in teaching or my relationship with the student teacher?

Kellett (1994) describes an approach to assessment of student teachers in the York University partnership which has many common features with other ITE partnership schemes involving HEIs. The York partnership approach achieves an effective reporting system on a student teacher's progress by the use of a commonly agreed framework for comment and assessment which allows for correlation of the views of HEI tutors, mentors and other teachers in the school. This correlation will normally result in some form of profile of the student teacher.

PROFILING AND ASSESSMENT

Since the TTA wishes to proceed with a competence-based Career Entry Profile scheme for all student teachers entering the profession in 1998, it will be useful for mentors to understand the issues surrounding profiles and profiling. A profile is not, in itself, a method of assessment even though competence-based approaches to teacher education tend to generate profile-based assessment formats (Jessup, 1991). Hutchinson (1994) details two early examples of profiles for entry into the profession which were used at the Roehampton Institute and Goldsmiths' College, London. It is obvious that HEIs and schools gather a great deal of information on students during their teaching practice and that this information has the potential to be a powerful resource for the detailed planning of school-based induction and even for future professional development in the early years of teaching. However, this information has rarely been passed to the school in which the student takes up a position. HEIs often used a pass/fail judgement which did not indicate how further professional development should take account of strengths and weaknesses already identified during the preparation of the teacher. In a profile, areas of a student teacher's strengths and weaknesses are identified to be addressed in the early years of teaching. Profiles are an attempt to make this information available for the first time. Profiling is an alternative to more traditional methods of assessment. The formative assessment process is the 'profiling' whilst the summative product is the 'profile'. Profiles are a means of recording assessments, but if the methods of assessment underpinning profiling are unsound then the profile will be also. Partnerships in ITE would need to review their assessment procedures before they introduced profiles.

There are clearly a number of problems with profiles highlighted by Husbands (1993) but this chapter will refer to only four. First, instead of being perceived as a partial statement about a Newly Qualified Teacher's competences and achievements, the TTA's profile eventually could be interpreted in such a way that QTS (Qualified Teacher Status) becomes a partial qualification. Already, there is evidence that schools expect too much from students in their first year (HMI, 1987) and the introduction of profiles will offer even tighter management and assessment of entrants to the profession. There is also the possibility that the TTA may integrate profiles and appraisal to produce lifelong personal profiles for all teachers. If this becomes the case then Day's (1995: 124) comment on teacher profiles is worth our consideration:

> Personal development profiles must be designed so that they foster the development of teachers as whole persons throughout their careers, recognising that, 'There is a natural connection between a person's work life and all other aspects of life' (Senge, 1990: 307) and, therefore, that personal mastery in all aspects of life must be supported; recognising that teachers are not technicians, but that teaching is bound up with their lives, their histories, the kind of persons they have been, and have become.

Second, it is not possible to produce a 'perfect' profile for there will be difficulties faced by the readers of such documents. Both the context and the reliability of profiles will in practice be open to a variety of interpretations. Profiles, however justified or accurate, become part of what teachers cannot control. Their purpose is to help management and enable and facilitate an assessment of the quality of the newly appointed member of staff. What they might come to represent within the world of competences and appraisal is beyond our ability to predict. There needs to be real support for professional development and genuine commitment to providing the resources to enhance the teaching capability of NQTs if profiles are to be of any real worth. Busher and Saran (1995) suggest that the current evidence indicates that this is unlikely to be the case. Since the introduction of financial delegation to schools, their managements have often taken steps to limit expenditure on staffing. The result has been that the number of less expensive support staff and part-time teachers has risen dramatically whilst the number of more experienced staff has declined. Between 1989 and 1994 the number of full-time teachers declined by 3 per cent whilst the number of part-time teachers rose by 26 per cent. These changes, including the decline in supply teachers, have raised considerable disquiet in schools. The idea that there will be adequate resources for the continued professional development of NQTs in schools is simply not believed by many in the profession. Competence-based profiles could also extend into the profession itself and be used for performance-related pay and promotion.

Third, profiles of the kind used in the TTA pilot scheme in 1996 are dominated by official teacher competence statements, which are centrally prescribed to give the impression of consistency. This prescriptive approach ignores the fact that the DfE had previously recognised that ITE partnerships had developed their own teacher competences. The profile should be a document that records the assessment of student teachers across a wide range of competences, both technical and personal qualities, but it should also allow mentors to interpret the competences and include references to professional values. Tomlinson (1995b) raises the further point that a teaching competence profile will allow for the specification of a range of teaching strategies and tactics so that there can be particular emphasis on certain subject areas. There is also the question of defining the exit competences of a beginning teacher for use in profiles. The University of Cambridge piloted a profile in 1989 and isolated and defined specific skills with competency descriptions of what a student teacher should be able to do at the end of the course, but abandoned it soon after because of the complications that arose. An important point is that competency- and profiling-based approaches are unable to record the internalising of certain values or, as Pring says, 'those that determine the quality of relationship between teachers and learners ... are being introduced into a professional community defined by social and ethical purposes, not merely a range of competences' (cited in Husbands, 1993: 122). Tomlinson (1995b) makes it clear that teaching qualities must include both competences and value commitments and that we can no longer call profiles competence profiles. They should be re-named 'teaching profiles' or 'teaching quality profiles'. The co-involvement of the student and mentor is an essential feature of the whole 'technical' part of assessment. It also points beyond itself to larger questions involving issues less susceptible to quantification or objective measurement.

Fourth, there is the question of the ownership of profiles. Whilst the TTA pilot Career Entry Profile stated that student teacher input was optional, it is likely that student teachers will have contributed substantially to these profiles and will have accumulated a variety of evidence in support of their progress which they will take with them to their new post. Will they eventually be used as references? Who will have access to them in schools? As Husbands (1993) says: 'profiling as a basis for the assessment of new entrants will remain chimeric'. The completion of the TTA profile document will be a joint responsibility between HEIs and partner schools. Student teachers are involved themselves in the process only if they choose to be so involved.

PROFESSIONAL VALUES AND ASSESSMENT

Many commentators on teacher education have concluded that we need to extend our definition of teacher competences beyond the purely technical, to the development of professional judgement and values. Values raise particular problems in assessment and are discussed in Chapter 3. Many have criticised competences and their use in teacher education because of their instrumentalist emphasis which fails to respect the value-laden or moral quality of teaching. We agree that 'know-how' and value commitments must be seen together. A more sophisticated notion of teaching quality was once implied in *Better Schools* (DES, 1985, par. 144) which argued that:

Like other professionals, teachers are expected to carry out their professional tasks in accordance with their judgement, without bias, precisely because they are professionals. This professionalism requires not only appropriate training and expertise but also the professional attitudes which give priority to the interests of those served and are constantly concerned to increase effectiveness through professional development.

What constitutes professional judgement and professional attitudes are questions that teachers need to revisit. Kerry and Shelton Mayes (1995) state that teachers 'need to acknowledge that assessment of the attainment of competences requires inferences to be made on the basis of a range of evidence: the less specific the criteria enunciated, the higher the level of inference will be, and the more informed judgement will be called for'. Obviously professional judgement will be structured by the teacher competences in use, but we need to remember that teaching involves both technical competence and professional judgement. It is easier to judge a lesson plan than whether a student has a commitment to professional values, such as the responsibility to promote equality of opportunity. Teaching is not a trade craft, but rather the teacher is a 'moral craftsperson', therefore competences for the teaching profession cannot be assessed with an exact degree of objectivity and accuracy. A student teacher's performance is intimately connected with the context, which, in teaching, is always value-laden. For example, it is important for mentors to assess whether or not student teachers respect confidentiality in their dealings with pupils; whether they co-operate with others in the success of the school; whether or not they exhibit professional responsibility for the resources of the school; whether they maintain a good rapport with parents and help communicate the purposes of the school to the wider community. These are the types of value questions which HEIs and schools should integrate into their competence-based courses. The Open University PGCE attempts to do this, as do the Northern Ireland teacher competences. There have also been important developments in NVQs, the original home of competences. 'Value Statements' have been produced for some courses to guide those assessing whether the candidates not only know the right thing but also whether they can do the right thing. This development is intended to give emphasis to the ethical dimension of the workplace. The University of East Anglia offers a B.Phil. (Teaching) for teachers early in their career which is specifically designed to encourage professional judgements and 'personal competences'. Everard (1995) has described how the Secondary Heads Association and Oxford Brookes University have included 'educational values' as a category of competence on their new headteacher course. Questions such as 'Do they show sympathy and tolerance for staff? Are they "people oriented"?' are addressed in this course. There is clearly a growing recognition and use of value aspects of personal competences.

We need to recognise that we cannot assess the intellectual and practical ability of student teachers without seeking to encompass professional values and commitments. Our aim must be to develop teachers with professional judgement, not mere competence. Tickle (1992) calls it 'the pursuit of practical wisdom'. However, we must not make the mistake of calling it 'common sense', for we often take values for granted and sometimes only become aware of them when we are personally challenged. Cooper and McIntyre (1996) emphasise that the cognitive and affective dimensions of the student teacher should always be considered together. The affective dimension of teaching concerns the establishment of a particular social climate in the classroom whilst the cognitive dimension of teaching focuses on the formal aspects of the curriculum. Craft knowledge for teaching, they claim, is informed by both dimensions. The claim is thus that 'good teaching' is necessarily an amalgam of skills and personal values, and an attempt to separate the two, to subordinate values to measurable competences, will grievously reduce quality in schools.

CONCLUSION

There is a clear need for a policy on assessment in teacher education which will be systematic and easily understood by student teachers and their mentors. This policy should stimulate and encourage all-round development, basing competences on a solid foundation of explicated professional values. Competence statements are important as a focus for diagnosis and help, but it should be recognised that any PGCE course can only provide a basic framework for successful teaching. This framework will need to be built on in practice, and in partnership with practising teachers, most particularly mentors. It will be seen that mentors require a clear guidance procedure on forming their own professional judgements of student teachers. Almost by definition, such partnership and assessment will need to be particular and specific to context, given a basic framework of competence. In other words, it should be local and 'bottom-up', not imposed 'top-down' by the DfEE. Such an imposition would reduce good teaching to lifeless conformity to a list of measurable factors recorded on profiles. It would justify the mistaken suggestion by Hargreaves (1989) that students should leave the course once they have reached certain threshold competences. As Whitty and Willmott (in Kerry and Shelton Mayes, 1995: 218) argue:

> the advantages of using a competence-based approach remain to be proven, and it seems unlikely to be the panacea that its staunchest advocates often imply. On the evidence of the courses we have seen so far, most institutions are at an early stage of development. . . . There is certainly insufficient experience to date to justify national imposition of any particular approach.

An additional danger of 'top-down' imposition is, of course, the proliferation of paperwork and unnecessary bureaucracy involved in an overprescriptive approach, a burden which would fall largely on mentors in schools.

More generally, however, mentors would be wise to retain a healthy scepticism towards all systems based purely on measurable factors. Bolton (1994: 455–457), in a speech to the National Commission on Education on 'The Quality and Training of Teachers' in 1992, identified the issues:

> What then are the characteristics of good teaching that impinge upon high quality learning by pupils and students? If they can be identified, can they be measured and/or assessed or appraised; and how, once identified, are they to be spread more widely through the system?

Like Newman, in the quotation at the head of this chapter, we can agree that not all human activity, particularly in education, can be 'weighed and measured' or result in some 'particular and narrow end'. However, we can also agree with Bolton that there are characteristics of good teaching which can be identified, and which we can seek to generalise. It is notable that the first characteristic in his list is that a good teacher should 'like children in general, though not all individual children equally, but set out to treat them all even-handedly'. It is interesting to speculate how the DfEE would measure such a basic factor in successful teaching, and what method of assessment could hope to capture this and many other elements similarly vital, but intangible.

3

A QUESTION OF VALUE,
OR VALUES?

There can be no democracy and, indeed, no freedom in a context where the most important aspects of life, and of education, namely those values which underpin both, are treated as given, as non-problematic and as not themselves subjects of continuing debate nor, as a consequence, open to modification and change.

(Kelly, 1995: xi)

INTRODUCTION

The discourse of government policy on teacher education and training in recent years has been conducted, for the most part, in terms of 'competences', 'skills' and 'outcomes'. Very little attention is paid officially to purpose, to questions of meaning, and the ends to which the pupils' acquired skills can be put. Almost as little attention is given to the wider purpose of the competences to be gained by the student teacher. The focus in the documentation is on what the teacher can do, rather than what the teacher is and can become: if the focus is on the teacher as needing to acquire certain skills, then 'training' is given in methods and techniques. The teacher is portrayed as a technician charged with specific tasks which are measurable in outcome, as one who is accountable to a manager assessing on the basis of the outcomes. How does such methodology meet the concept of professional values?

This question, of course, itself begs two further questions: 'What is a profession?' and 'What do we mean by values?' The first of these questions is discussed below briefly and elsewhere in this chapter. The meaning of 'values' in moral and social contexts takes us into a wide philosophical debate which we do not have the time to address in this discussion. Readers are referred to McLaughlin's (1994) short introduction to the meaning and place of values in education. In this chapter we will use a simple practical definition: values are the complex sets of beliefs which it is considered positive and appropriate for teachers to hold, and the actions by which those beliefs may be communicated to pupils.

IS TEACHING A PROFESSION?

This may seem a paradoxical question to many teachers, and yet it is interesting to note that teaching is the only professional group in England and Wales which does not have a self-governing representative body to regulate it. The legal, medical and para-medical professions all have bodies which regulate entry, set minimum standards of professional knowledge and represent their members. Most importantly, each of them has the power to exclude from the profession not only on the basis of incompetence but for the violation of a code of professional ethics. The General Medical Council, for example, can legally bar an individual practising medicine in England and Wales for an act which is not in itself illegal, but a violation of ethics. Even 'fringe' activities such as public relations have an official code of ethical practice; teachers have not.

A profession can be defined by the recognition of the social and moral context of its work. To accept a model of the teacher as one who only systematically *transmits* knowledge is to deny the professionalism of the teacher, and to reduce teacher education to the production of skilled technicians comparable to the proliferating variety of computer experts. If, on the other hand, we focus on the teacher as professional, we need to address issues about human development and the purpose of education. It is our contention that these issues, far from being marginal, are in fact at the centre of teacher education, and that without them teaching becomes a mechanical skill, which is unable to 'deliver', promote or enhance the personal, social and moral development which the government professes to favour. It is in this context that subject mentors and student teachers may begin to approach the question of professional values.

The idea that teaching can be narrowly based on producing quantifiable learning outcomes, which constitute the major criterion of teaching competence, is highly questionable. The teacher is not simply one whose contribution is limited to the systematic transmission of knowledge in a school. The demonstration of professional values goes beyond the demonstration of classroom competence. By concentrating on practical teaching skills and methods – the mechanics of teaching – it is possible to produce a teacher who is able to manage a class and instruct pupils with a fair show of competence. However, professional teachers are aware of the larger social setting, have the flexibility to anticipate change, to adapt their methods to new demands, and sometimes to challenge the requirements laid upon them. To produce such professional teachers, subject mentors should attempt to strike a balance between a focus on the development of competence and raising their student teachers' awareness about the meaning of their task. This may be achieved by encouraging student teachers to see their daily teaching in the perspective of larger theories of human development and social policy, for it should always be remembered that the teacher is also 'educator' – one who helps form human beings. Therefore, competences must exist within a framework of the personal values and qualities appropriate to the teaching profession. Student teachers need to be encouraged to develop a commitment to professional values which they are able to demonstrate through their personal example. Newly Qualified Teachers, therefore, require not only competence but professional value commitments.

The centrality of values

Values are an integral part of teaching, reflected in what is taught and also in how teachers teach, and interact with, pupils. Pupils spend the greatest amount of their daily time with teachers, who have significant opportunities to influence them. The time spent by pupils in the company of teachers is, therefore, inevitably formative. Intentionally or not, teachers shape the character of pupils, for at the heart of the practice of education is the relationship between teacher and pupil. It is this relationship which sets the tone for all else in the classroom. As Kelly (1995: 105) reminds us, 'The provision of education is both a moral and a practical imperative in a democratic society.' It is, therefore, astonishing that teaching lacks a professional and distinctive code of ethics which focuses on the interests of pupils. The very purpose of schools is to make a difference to the lives of pupils and so the moral and ethical dimensions of teaching provide the core value context in which teachers are located. Values are central to competent professional practice,

47

but competence-based models of teacher training are widely believed to have no commitment to professional values (Hyland, 1993). That is why there is growing interest in defining and assessing ethical judgement and values in the professional training of teachers.

The attempt to encapsulate the full range of human abilities and adaptations within the concept of competence is simply not possible. As Strain (1995: 47–48) observes:

> Professionality is inextricably bound up with widely shared values, understandings and attitudes regarding the social order and the rules by which others, in certain relationships, may instigate a claim on us . . . to claim the standing of a professional has come to mean adherence to an ethic, a moral principle, which derives from a freely undertaken commitment to serve others as individual human beings, worthy of respect, care and attention.

Teaching is above all a 'self-giving' enterprise concerned with the betterment or good of pupils. Since values are embedded in the standards by which subject mentors assess and help develop student teachers, there is clearly scope for systematic assessment of competent professional practice in teaching within a values context.

At present teacher 'training' appears to be sliding into a world of totally instrumental purposes in which *explicit* values disappear. However, competences are not value-free, they are *implicitly* instrumental and that is why their meaning should be clearly displayed and their ramifications explored. The aim of the teacher training competence model is to realise some predetermined goal which is often treated as unproblematic in discussion and operation. It is clear that if one includes attitudinal or value dimensions in competences then the criteria of achievement are not so easily identifiable. Bland statements of professional values, which receive general agreement, are rarely associated with tangible outcomes or with actual activities undertaken by teachers in school. Some lists of competences include personal attributes which demand considerable sensitivity in assessment, for example in the Northern Ireland model outlined in Chapter 1.

Nevertheless, we believe it is necessary to set the stage for ideas and suggestions to emerge from within the teaching profession itself. The profession needs to generate the teaching principles to which teachers would wish their actions to conform. The word 'professional' in teaching is increasingly being viewed as meaning simply skill and efficiency. The role of the subject mentor, therefore, should include support for classroom teaching which goes beyond the mechanics of teaching, for a concern for values can and should be part of subject area teaching. The conception of professional values and responsibility in teaching is too narrow when restricted to technological criteria of functional success.

Teachers are also role models, and it follows that, when, in the classroom, a student teacher exhibits values or personal characteristics which are held to be at variance with what it is educationally desirable for pupils to acquire, then there is cause for concern. Part of the subject mentor's work can be to help student teachers to recognise, acquire and practise professional values in their teaching. The aim should be to socialise the student teacher into the profession and into its values as a profession. Subject mentors have the responsibility of helping student teachers to think open-mindedly about the many basic values involved in the teaching contexts that they experience. After all, teaching is located within a set of beliefs, values, habits, traditions and ways of thinking that are shared and understood by those already in the profession, but which are seldom articulated. Similarly, subject mentors should also be aware that all student teachers bring with them a unique personality and set of attitudes, skills and preferences. Unquestionably, subject mentors will influence the development of the professional and personal identities of student teachers. In the absence of any professional code of ethics for teaching, it is important that we look at, and comment on, what government and its agencies have said in the last ten years about the role of teachers in regard to values, in particular in the preparation of teachers.

OFFICIAL VIEWS OF TEACHING

The requirements of the Education Reform Act of 1988 place a duty on all teachers to promote the 'spiritual, moral, social' education of their pupils and yet the teacher training competences in England and Wales give only passing reference to these areas. The determination of the government to uphold certain values, often expressed in platitudes (for example, as the nebulous 'spiritual and moral development' of pupils in schools), and the gulf between the values of the government and those held by many teachers has led to confusion about the expectations that are now being placed upon teachers. Sir Ron Dearing's revision of the National Curriculum 'successfully' excised practically all references to the values content of subjects; this has resulted in reinforcing the assumption that what teachers really need is more expertise in the subject they teach. As O'Hear (1988) says: 'Having a qualification in one's subject and actually teaching in a school are all that is relevant.' The values dimension of teachers' knowledge is either ignored or trivialised in this viewpoint for it assumes that caring for pupils is an everyday activity for which no special education or skill is required. In other words, anyone with a degree can become a teacher.

The characteristics that differentiate and define teaching do not necessarily imply the criteria for good teaching, successful teaching or even effective teaching. Successful teaching is simply teaching which brings about the desired learning in narrow subject terms. Effective teaching is determined objectively by the nature of the subject itself and how best to teach it. Good teaching is harder to discern and is, therefore, open to wider interpretations. It has long been accepted that good teaching is much wider than the transmission of knowledge. The idea of the 'good teacher' takes on richer meaning if it is viewed as someone who is capable of expressing care and respect; who takes the pupils seriously and finds what is good in his or her pupils.

There is a fear among teacher educators that the competence-based arrangements for initial teacher training in the context of England and Wales are weakening the link between theory and practice. The Council for the Accreditation of Teacher Education (CATE) was commissioned by the Department of Education and Science (DES) to improve teaching quality and it was given responsibility for advice about, and the specification and implementation of, the criteria which ITE courses awarding Qualified Teacher Status (QTS) should meet. CATE concentrated its attention on three areas of teacher competence: (a) academic knowledge; (b) professional skills; and (c) personal qualities. Whilst (a) and (b) received detailed attention, (c) was left to some basic guidance on the requirements expected of candidates at interview. Her Majesty's Inspectorate (HMI) did comment on the qualities of good teachers by observing that reliability, punctuality, co-operation and a willingness to take on essential tasks were important.

The DES (1989b) gave its view when it made it clear that candidates for teaching should be checked for their 'personal and intellectual qualities ... and their physical and mental fitness to teach'. No attempt was made to define what is meant by personal qualities. Circular 24/89 specified five limited criteria for the personal qualities of potential candidates for teacher training: a sense of responsibility; a robust but balanced outlook; sensitivity; enthusiasm; and a facility in communication. A rather sketchy outline by any standards. Circular 9/92 is widely seen by commentators as inadequate for defining the complexities of professional values and expertise in two major areas: reflection, and moral and ethical judgements. At the very end of the circular's list of competences, under the heading of Further Professional Development, it merely notes that student teachers should have a 'readiness to promote the moral and spiritual well being of pupils'.

Such developments have limited the scope of the debate about professional values and purposes in education because of the overemphasis on the behavioural aspects in the competences. Pring (1992: 17) has commented that

> These conditions make little mention of theory. They require no philosophical insights. They demand no understanding of how children are motivated; they attach little importance to the social context in which the school functions – unless it be that of local business and the world of work; they attach no significance to historical insight into the present; they have no place for the ethical formulation of those who are to embark on this, the most important of all moral undertakings.

Pring is making the point that the ethical intuition of good teachers is frequently as important as their subject-area knowledge and teaching skill. Carr (1993a) has also commented that

> The crude and artificial separation of competences from attitudes reinforces the false impression that what we are solely concerned with in the professional preparation of teachers is a kind of *training* in repertoires of uncontroversial skills and dispositions when what such preparation should be truly concerned with is the *education* of professional capacities to address rationally issues which, on any correct view of the logic of educational discourse, are deeply controversial and problematic.

Carr's views on competences will be revisited in this chapter, especially since he advocates a return to non-competence-based programmes of teacher education.

Cross-curricular dimensions

The National Curriculum Council (NCC) published at least two documents which have direct relevance for the professional values of teachers. Curriculum Guidance No. 8, *Education for Citizenship* (NCC, 1990), emphasises the cross-curricular nature of certain values which teachers in all subject areas need to address. All teachers are asked to ensure that they are able to teach the nature and basis of duties, responsibilities and rights and also to promote positive attitudes about the value of democracy, developing personal moral codes and exploring pupil values and beliefs. The NCC's 1993 publication *Spiritual and Moral Development* made the following statement:

> Values are inherent in teaching. Teachers are by the nature of their profession 'moral agents' who imply values by the way they address pupils and each other, the way they dress, the language they use and the effort they put into their work.

This statement has been severely attacked by Carr, who says that it has little to offer teachers on the nature and extent of the moral education role of the teacher. He describes the statement as vacuous and consisting of simple platitudes (Carr, 1993b). Nevertheless, the statement at least draws attention to the human dimension of teaching, which makes all the more noticeable the omission of such values in the criteria for training teachers.

The Office for Standards in Education's (OFSTED, 1993) *Handbook for the Inspection of Schools* calls for the inspection of pupils' response to teaching by means of observations of the quality of relationships in the school and the respect between pupils and teachers. Questions such as whether the school teaches the principles which distinguish right from wrong and whether pupils relate positively to each other will be asked by those inspecting. Does the school foster values such as honesty, fairness and respect for truth and justice? It is difficult enough for OFSTED to inspect the cognitive domain in schools – in the affective domain some think it impossible. Naylor (1996) comments that teachers feel apprehensive about inspection in this area and he refers to the 'shambolic OFSTED guidelines' relating to the values dimension in schools and in teaching.

THE TEACHER TRAINING AGENCY

In September 1994 the DfE transferred responsibility for funding, quality and policy in ITT from the Higher Education Funding

Council (HEFC) to the Teacher Training Agency (TTA). The new agency's view on the values inherent within teaching can be seen in the pilot *Career Entry Profile for Newly Qualified Secondary Teachers* issued by the TTA in January 1996. The pilot profile simply assesses student teachers on showing 'readiness to promote the spiritual and moral'. A competent NQT 'plans and evaluates pupils' moral, spiritual, social and cultural development. Identifies and acts upon specific targets for personal development.' Again, no further guidelines are given to subject mentors who may have to operate these profiles. In the TTA draft document *Quality of Teaching and Assessment* of March 1996, the only reference to the promotion of explicit values is made in relation to an understanding of issues about equal opportunities policies and practices in the professional context. The TTA has not shown itself to date to be much interested in the professional values dimension of teaching.

This contrasts with the work of the School Curriculum and Assessment Authority (SCAA), which replaced the NCC. SCAA established a national forum on values in the community and education in 1996, representing many constituencies including business, the media, the law, social services, religious groups, youth workers, researchers, parents and teachers. One of the greatest concerns of the forum was teacher education – both initial and in-service. It found that HEIs had no common understanding of what constituted the moral and spiritual in education and that cross-curricular dimensions in these areas were not working. Since it might be argued that society in general appears to be confused on such issues, it is not surprising to find that HEIs were equally in the dark. Nevertheless, the forum felt concern that the TTA did not appear to take much notice of these areas and it recommended that spiritual and moral values be incorporated into the competences for teacher 'training'.

Many of the statements about values made in the last ten years by the DES, DfE, DfEE, CATE, NCC, TTA, OFSTED and SCAA have had little concrete application to teacher education, and certainly do not provide subject mentors with the necessary information or skills successfully to mentor student teachers in these important areas. Their combined effect and the introduction of the competences in teacher education has been to remove academic courses in the psychology, philosophy, sociology and history of education. In the search for relevance few ITE courses would even describe themselves as 'theoretically informed' (Whiting *et al.*, 1996).

Questions about a school's educational purposes have been neglected, as the focus is on cost effectiveness, which it seems is justified by the quality and standards revealed by measurable outcomes. There is an increase in the technical element of teachers' work and a reduction in the professional aspects, as schools and teacher education are increasingly regulated by external agencies. These agencies do not seem to confer effectively with each other in producing a coherent and intelligible statement about how teacher competences relate to the value dimensions of teaching. Perhaps this is an impossible task for State agencies to undertake?

The confusion in government and government-agency documentation is a direct consequence of the lack of genuine consultation with teachers and teacher educators. Many believe that if teachers had a General Teaching Council with an ethics committee it would be possible to produce a statement of values or ethics which might be implemented in schools. Teachers are already doing a great deal to ensure that pupils understand the difference between right and wrong, sometimes against parents who are unwilling or unable to support the moral work of schools. The fact that in a MORI poll in 1996 teachers were seen as the best moral example to the young, above religious leaders, politicians and pop singers, is an indication of both the role teachers are believed to have in the moral education of young people and of their professional standing. We need to explore how this relates to the actual practice of professional values in the classroom.

PROFESSIONAL VALUES IN THE CLASSROOM

Teachers are still a major influence on pupils and the values they form. These values are reflected in what teachers choose to permit or encourage, for the values of a teacher are clearly reflected in the life of the classroom. The way a teacher insists on accuracy in the work of pupils, or responds to their interests, conveys values which are clearly being introduced to those pupils. Teachers represent the school's philosophy to the pupil and the larger public. A teacher cannot be entirely *neutral,* for pupils need the example of those who are not indifferent. They need teachers who are full of enthusiasms and commitments in their teaching. All the time teachers are teaching they are under examination by their pupils. Their characters are analysed; their fairness examined; their inconsistencies probed. Teaching is clearly a test of character for a student teacher. The teacher is a model of what it is to be a human being for pupils and no amount of competence in the class will avail if the teacher is not an appropriate model.

Teaching is a moral science, for as Elliott (1989: 9) proposes:

> When teachers are viewed as practitioners of an ethic then they may be described appropriately as members of a *profession*. But when their activity is viewed as a kind of technology then their status may simply be reduced to that of the technician.

In addition, Tom (1980) has concluded that

> Teaching is moral in at least two senses. On the one hand, the act of teaching is moral because it presupposes that something of value is to be taught (Peters, 1965). On the other hand, the teacher–student relationship is inherently moral because of its inequality. This relationship, notes Hawkins (1973), entails 'an offer of control by one individual over the functioning of another, who in accepting this offer, is tacitly assured that control will not be exploitative but will be used to enhance the competence and extend the independence of the one controlled ...'. Those who adhere to the applied science metaphor are insensitive to the moral dimension of teaching because their primary focus is on increasing the efficiency and effectiveness of teaching.

Teaching by this view is a moral craft. The adoption of a moral perspective on teaching does not, however, mean that one can abandon learning outcomes.

Much has been written on the area of values in teaching, not least by White (1990), who describes early education as the 'formation of dispositions'. Wilson (1993: 113) also speaks of moral dispositions when he says:

> Moral qualities are directly relevant to any kind of classroom practice: care for the pupil, enthusiasm for the subject, conscientiousness, determination, willingness to co-operate with colleagues and a host of others. Nobody, at least on reflection, really believes that effective teaching – let alone effective education – can be reduced to a set of skills; it requires certain dispositions of character. The attempt to avoid the question of what these dispositions are by emphasising pseudo-practical terms like 'competences' or 'professional' must fail.

The argument here is that teachers must provide support for classroom learning which goes beyond the mere mechanics of teaching. Elsewhere, Eraut (1994) argues that teachers have a moral commitment to serve the interests of their pupils by reflecting on their well-being and their progress and deciding how best these can be fostered or promoted. By so doing they contribute to the moral shaping of what pupils become. As Sockett (1993: 14) observes: 'many teachers have a moral vision, a moral sense, and a moral motive however mixed up they may be in any individual'. How much of this is recognised in teacher training? Elbaz (1992) believes that we do not pay enough attention to this aspect of teacher education and training as a result of our 'technocratic mind set'. Goodlad *et al.* (1990) go further, commenting that we need to address a fundamental void in the preparation of teachers:

> Teaching is fundamentally a moral enterprise in which adults ask and require children to change in directions chosen by the adults. Understanding teaching in this light confronts a teacher with potentially unsettling questions: By what authority do I push for change in the lives of these children? At what costs to their freedom and autonomy? Where does my responsibility for these young lives begin and end? How should I deal with true moral dilemmas in which it is simply not possible to realise two goals or avoid two evils? How much pain and discomfort am I willing to endure on behalf of my student teachers? How are my own character flaws affecting the lives of others?

All of this means more work for the teacher and it can be a difficult and thankless task. We need to consider how well students are currently prepared to meet these questions.

A question of professionalism

There are many who believe that the present arrangements for teacher education undermine the teaching profession and that it is time to reassert the professionalism of teachers (Avis, 1994). Downie (1990), for example, believes that the teaching profession should be seen as service through relationships and that teachers have a duty to speak out on matters of social justice and social utility. He also believes that teachers should be educated rather than trained, on the basis that educated persons remain interested in their subject and think it worthwhile to pursue it, the mechanics of teaching being no substitute for their knowledge. Hoyle and John (1995) have said much about the responsibility of teachers which goes beyond accountability or simply meeting the requirements of a set of procedures. With regard to the qualities of a teacher, they list a number, professing that teachers should be: tolerant, patient, gentle, sympathetic, socially conscious and responsible. Subject mentors would no doubt look for and expect similar qualities in their student teachers. A danger, however, is the development of an 'omnicompetent model' of teaching in which the expectations of the teacher's role are extremely extensive.

Obviously, any view of ethics for teaching should have broad public and professional support. Nevertheless, teachers need to possess a set of virtues as the teacher's moral practice in teaching is something to be emulated. As Strike (1995) says, the way the teacher talks and behaves is taken by pupils as a basis for how they should behave. Carr (1993b) criticises teacher training competences for presenting teaching as a relatively value-free technological enterprise, concerned solely with the delivery of a prescribed curriculum. He believes that teachers should be viewed as 'better' people and have certain virtues. A problem here may be the personal life of teachers, and whether this can conflict with their duties as teachers. He concludes that most problems in the professional sphere call for a 'moral rather than a technical response' and that practice needs to be characterised in 'terms of virtues rather than skills'. Clearly, this places a considerable moral burden on teachers, of which student teachers will need to be made aware.

THE PRACTICE OF PROFESSIONAL VALUES

What are the practices that will facilitate ethical competence among teachers? The ethical dimension of teaching cannot be located in any particular element or at any specific moment of educational activity; rather, it should affect the whole person. It would be difficult for any one person to compile a list of practices that would be accepted by the teaching profession. Neville (1993) has compiled a Shared Values Charter for comprehensive schools in which each member of the school community is encouraged to respect, and use opportunities to serve, others. The Charter emphasises the equal value of all persons, openness, participation, co-operation, development of the whole person, and empowerment. The Charter is rather broad and would need to be tailored to each particular school.

However, professional values in teaching can be demonstrated through the teacher's respect for pupils as individuals. In the area of relationships with pupils alone a whole series of ethical/value competences can be described. Teachers, including student teachers, will wish to encourage honesty in pupils and will seek to encourage them to tell the truth. Above all, teachers will always ensure that pupils come first; that they will care for them and always try to find what is good in them; they will treat them seriously and consider their interests; they will help them gain self-respect and will understand in their teaching that pupils are often frightened by the level of difficulty of their work, and especially by the consequences of their inability to learn things they do not understand. Teachers will help pupils to make a real effort by consciously ensuring that they have a sense of achievement. Teachers will listen to pupils, they will praise them, they will be available for them and focus on their success. Teachers will be models of interpersonal relations.

Other value areas, which could be subdivided to create statements indicating what teachers should be expected to do, include: positive relationships with other teachers and parents; regard for equal opportunities and consideration for others; involvement with ethical issues and helping to resolve the value conflicts of pupils; commitment to professional development and developing a sense of professional judgement; sense of responsibility for personal and collective actions. There are no doubt other areas, but there is a case for student teachers explicitly illustrating these values during their school experience.

Chappell and Hager (1994) make the case that teacher competences which ignore values, including ethical and personal qualities, are not worth using. They adopt an integrated approach to producing descriptions of practices which can capture the ethical and value positions of a profession. Values are posed as informal learning practices which characterise the initiation of new teachers into the teaching profession. Some of these are immeasurable but Chappell and Hager make a strong case for the assessment of values. They state that the idea of empathy for pupils in the abstract is difficult to describe and assess, but that in a classroom situation one could make a judgement. They propose that 'by describing attributes and activities in an integrated and contextualised way, long standing difficulties associated with arbitrary and idiosyncratic "hidden assessments" of individuals, which often have characterised values assessment in the workplace, can be avoided'. Further, they suggest that teachers should themselves compile lists of professional value practices for the classroom and school. This method could be applied to the teacher competences in Circular 9/92, or the competences used by ITT institutions, in order to emphasise the role of the values dimension in teacher education. It will be seen that the mentor has available a range of possible actions in promoting the importance of professional values to student teachers.

MENTORING AND PROFESSIONAL VALUES

The role of subject mentoring itself involves modelling good practice in the widest sense: in particular, the values of the profession. Student teachers will look to the subject mentor for advice and assistance on what will be expected from them in terms of school routines, relationships with pupils and staff and, usually, the subject mentor will be the first port of call when the student teacher has any difficulty, which may include personal problems. The student teacher will generally follow or even emulate the practice of the subject mentor, especially at the early stages of teaching experience, so it is important that the subject mentor realises this possibility and, as far as is possible, presents the highest standards of teaching and professional practice to the student teacher.

The student teacher is in the process of becoming a member of the teaching profession and he or she will need to understand and implement school policies including the Mission Statement, or Statement of Values of the school. The subject mentor might wish to spend time on these areas and discuss them with the student teacher. At the same time, the subject mentor might usefully undertake to talk about the ethos or life of the school with the student teacher, go through the customs and practices of the school, and the kind of expectations which there will be of the student teacher from both staff and pupils. These aspects of school life are often learned by student teachers informally as they proceed through their teaching experience, but they would more effectively form part of any induction programme for new student teachers and even new staff in a school. Student teachers have to accept the standards and principles of membership of the school community in order to serve its purposes. Rutter et al. (1979) have shown that the culture or ethos of a school has a greater effect on pupils' behaviour than does the academic curriculum – it must also have an effect on teachers.

Subject values

A much more complex area involves the values dimensions of particular subject areas. Some subject areas obviously have a more direct relationship to the values question than others, but none is exempt. Every subject teacher needs to be aware of the requirement to promote the betterment of their pupils and this can also be achieved through curricular areas. In mathematics, for example, subject mentors might ask student teachers to consider: How are the examples they use constructed? What values are implicit in the contexts? Is there any bias in the example? Such 'values questions' encourage reflection on the moral aspects of teaching. In the same way the science mentor may ask student teachers whether they encourage pupils to consider the impact on society of scientific advancement.

The same might be applied to particular teaching methods. If subject mentors accept that there is a moral dimension to the teacher's role, then they may be able to suggest the nature of the values dimension in their subject area. For example, what may be effective teaching for some, say, teaching science at the learning pace of the most able, may at the same time be morally questionable for those who cannot keep up. It is these types of issues that student teachers need to consider and link to professional values. Another could be whether someone having a sound knowledge of their subject but no respect for what they are teaching is acceptable in the teaching profession. Do student teachers need to display a love of their subject?

Subject mentors should be aware also that student teachers bring their own sets of values, attitudes and emotions to the school and to their teaching. Student teachers often show fear, and experience both failure and success in their teaching and staff relationships. In their contacts with pupils, student teachers can experience stress and be extremely nervous. Subject mentors have a responsibility here to support student teachers, especially in the early stages of their school experience.

Subject mentors will, however, recognise that student teachers will need emotional maturity, which is linked inextricably to the acquisition of, and use of, classroom competences. Subject mentors will be asking: Are they adequate role models for the pupils? Are they patient with pupils? Are they selfish or generous with their time? How do they behave with other teachers? Student teachers' main example in attempting to answer these questions is often by reference to subject mentors themselves. Again, the role of subject mentoring places emphasis on the professional value commitments of subject mentors. This is why it is important that subject mentors, whilst being guided by their intuitions and assumptions, should not take them for granted. Subject mentors should allow student teachers to question them to establish how teachers examine the values dimension of their own subject teaching. Chapter 5 discusses discursive mentoring practices which allow such exploration. It is this openness which will encourage a professional relationship in which the student teacher will learn.

Professional qualities

In the Open University PGCE course student teachers are required to demonstrate professional qualities in the way that teaching competence is displayed. The idea is that student teachers should recognise that teaching includes the demonstration of professional qualities and values that go beyond the demonstration of classroom competence. The OU course does not allow mentors to 'tick off' competences in a discrete way. However, how competences and professional values are actually fused is not clear and the list of professional value commitments is somewhat limited. Student teachers are to demonstrate values through 'personal example and their role in school' but it is not really made clear how this is assessed (Moon and Shelton Mayes, 1995). As Norris (1991) observes, an action seen as competent will partly depend on the audience judging it, and she goes on to say that 'The trouble with competence is that it now has a currency way beyond its operational reach'. Like the Northern Ireland model, the Open University model of teacher education does at least recognise the importance of professional values, and gives some guidelines on how professional values and competences can be integrated in order to help student teachers both reflect on and practise these values in their teaching.

In general, there have been two approaches to competence, described by Whitty and Willmott (1991). First, competence is seen as an ability to perform a task satisfactorily, the task being defined and the criteria for success set out. Second, competence is seen as wider than the first approach, encompassing attitudinal dimensions and professional values. In this second view neither the competence nor the criteria of achievement are so readily susceptible to sharp and discrete identification. This raises particular problems of assessment which the Open University course must have. However, it is exactly this type of approach which attempts to avoid the narrow technical and purely instrumental approach of using the teacher competences as tools on their own, and subject mentors will need to be aware of this issue and reflect creatively on its importance.

REFLECTION AND PROFESSIONAL VALUES

The terms 'reflection' and 'critical reflection' are increasingly appearing in the descriptions of approaches to teacher education. They are commonly found in the Whiting *et al.* (1996) survey of teacher education. Many argue (see Chapter 4) that reflection is an essential professional attribute, for it should enable teachers to respond quickly and appropriately to changing circumstances and maintain a critical perspective on their teaching. Reflection in practice could be defined as the conscientious and systematic review of the aims, plans, actions and evaluation of teaching in order to reinforce effectiveness. The question, however, is not whether student teachers should be encouraged to reflect; it is what they should be encouraged to be reflective about. Bridges and Kerry (1993) insist that the values dimension of teaching should be a focus for student teachers, and warn against any model of reflection which 'ignores the role of experience in the development of the situational knowledge and value base which inform intelligent professional judgement'. Avis (1994) believes that since the idea of the 'reflective practitioner' works within the notion of good practice it can, paradoxically, be reduced to a technicist model, as the word 'practitioner' emphasises 'competence'. However, a case might be made against such analysis as the term clearly has its roots in the language of 'action research' and 'reflective practice'. Perhaps a more useful way to describe a reflective teacher might be *reflective professional*, wherein the use of 'professional' gives increased weight to values which surround, inform and are informed by 'reflection'.

The research by Tickle (1996) would indicate that student teachers reflect mainly on the technicalities of teaching performance, which is focused on problem-solving and developing strategies which 'work' in the classroom. He found that aims and values underlying practice barely entered the realms of reflective consciousness, let alone becoming subject to any scrutiny and critique. He concludes:

> If the predominant assumptions in teacher education systems, as well as among individual teachers, are about the need to

achieve efficient performance in observable, 'workable' technical and clinical skills, then it may be that Schön's (1983) notion of reflective practice will remain limited to thoughts about procedural matters and the means of effective teaching. Or it may be used simply, as an implicit tacit aim. The more fundamental and educationally necessary focus on the purposes and values of education, including those of teacher education, may continue to elude not just these teachers but the teaching community in general.

It has been argued (Calderhead, 1987) that reflection among student teachers is often not 'critical' and can easily focus on simple descriptive evaluations of technical skills or processes. Elsewhere it has been claimed that reflective practice has become a catchphrase on which many teacher education courses hang their own philosophy (Quicke, 1996). And yet for Carr (1993c) 'it is impossible truly to formulate any serious policies in education without some rational moral reflection upon the goals of human flourishing to which it is directed. Such reflection is also, of course, an occasion for the development of attitudes which should express themselves in a real moral commitment to these goals.' He concludes that the knowledge and understanding which should properly inform the professional consciousness of the competent teacher is 'rooted in rational reflection about educational policies and practices and what is ethically, as well as instrumentally, appropriate to achieve them'. It is this which is often lacking in teacher education courses, for the research evidence would indicate that student teachers do not, on the whole, reflect on the values dimension of teaching very much. It is important, therefore, that subject mentors keep the issue of reflection always before the student teachers for whom they are responsible. How can the mentor assist student teachers in this area?

VALUING THE PROFESSION

Socrates believed that the role of education is to make people both intelligent and good. The aim of teacher education today is to prepare skilled teachers, with the emphasis on competence. Teachers should also foster the good, for education is a moral business. Alasdair McIntyre (1981) calls our attention to Aristotle's *Ethics* as an alternative source for a rationale for moral education. In *The Ethics* Aristotle's voice is more than his own as he constantly asks, 'What

63

do we say?' not 'What do I say?' This collective voice is that of the shared norms and values of society and contrasts sharply with the individualistic voice typical of our present time. Our inability to say 'we' in making moral prescriptions reflects a lack of a genuine moral consensus and sense of moral community. As we have already said, at the heart of education is the relationship between teacher and pupil and at the heart of any school community is the ability to speak for the community's shared values and moral norms.

McIntyre (1985) takes a pessimistic view of teaching in that he says: 'Teachers are the forlorn hope of the culture of Western modernity . . . for the mission [with] which contemporary teachers are entrusted is both essential and impossible.' It is impossible, he claims, because we have no standards of rational objectivity and we have no agreement even on what standards are. This argument has some force to it, but it does not mean that we should abandon our search for the values and standards of a good teacher. It is important that teachers and lecturers recognise the 'problematic nature of knowledge, of values and thus of the practice of education itself' (Kelly, 1995: 136) by examining their own practice in terms of its goals as well as its methods. If student teachers are to be inducted into a profession whose value commitments are explicit, a professional ethical code for teaching will be required. It also means that the teacher competences, viewed and operated as instrumental tools, cannot be an acceptable basis for training or educating future teachers.

Hoyle (1995: 60) has commented that one view is that 'To be "professional" is to have acquired a set of skills through competency-based training which enables one to deliver efficiently according to contract a customer-led service in compliance with accountability procedures collaboratively implemented and managerially assured.' He admits that this definition may exaggerate the views of those who perceive teachers fundamentally as technicians, but Bonnett (1996) says it is not sufficient for teachers simply to say that this competence-based training model is inappropriate because it does not accord with their underlying conception of education. He says that it is precisely their underlying conception of education that is being called into question by the political powers that be.

The instrumental values contained in the competences are designed to bring about a complete reorientation with regard to the fundamental values in education. The significance of the substitution of the word 'training' for 'education' in regard to teacher preparation has not yet emerged. There is a mood of distrust among teachers about government intentions in teacher education, and much else besides. Teacher training has certainly become more like a school-based apprenticeship in which theory is excluded and even reflection is limited to improving technical competences.

School and society

There are many pressures working against those seeking to educate pupils with moral principles, not least the mass media and advertising which have helped to create a synthetic culture of consumption. Following the introduction of the Parents' Charter, it may appear that some parents and pupils have developed a stronger sense of their own rights than of their responsibilities. Such a belief, perhaps, underpinned the proposal in October 1996 by both the government and the opposition for contracts between school and parents, which would articulate the rights and responsibilities of all parties involved in the education of children. An example of the ramifications of such a climate occurred when a student teacher was verbally abused in a school hall by a group of pupils, but the student teacher decided that she did not wish to report it. When asked by the subject mentor why she did not report the incident, she responded by saying that there had been no witnesses. While it is not unusual for some student teachers to experience a reluctance to be identified as 'authority figures', it is clear that the traditional moral authority of the teacher is reduced to a narrow, legalistic authority when student teachers begin to think like this. It also says something about the lack of explicit professional standards for teachers.

Whilst teachers need to be careful about any *imposition* of values in schools, they cannot avoid *values in teaching*. That is why it is important that the values in the act of teaching are clearly described and understood. Ultimately, it is the family which is the main social agency for helping young people, but the goals of a school inevitably will refer to character development even if such references are limited explicitly to encouraging pupils to strive for personal success and to being of service to the community. The ethic of the professional teacher is different from that of the parent, but, ideally, it should be seen as one which complements it. Parents, according to the 1996 MORI poll, trust teachers and consider them to be the best moral examples for their children, which is a heavy responsibility.

CONCLUSION

It will be seen from the previous discussion that the role of the subject mentor in this area is perhaps the most difficult of all the obligations included in the function. This is for many reasons, not least the perceived lack of an agreed moral consensus within English society itself. More broadly, however, the difficulty lies in the fact that government has consciously and systematically sought to impose a model of 'good teaching', which is defined almost entirely in instrumental terms, as the achievement of a set of measurable outcomes. This model sits uneasily with any model which takes 'education' to be a process of eliciting the balanced and harmonious development of children, not least in terms of their social, moral and spiritual development. It is very easy to envisage situations where these two models clash, in particular where less able pupils are concerned. Situations will arise where a subject mentor and student teacher may have to engage in serious moral reflection on how far compliance with the 'official model' may be taken, where it is damaging to the interests of the pupils concerned. This necessarily involves a risk to the career of the student teacher if taken as a fundamental critique of the 'measurable outcomes' world view, and one which needs to be carefully considered.

The last two decades have seen the most determined attempt to reduce teaching to a technical function since 'payment by results' and the 'pupil–teacher system' were instituted in the nineteenth century. We would argue that, in this situation, the subject mentor should, to the greatest extent possible, keep alive the humane concept of teaching as personal communication of values, as well as knowledge, understanding and skills:

> For if teachers are not merely to be agents through whose activities the values of the dominant group in society are imposed upon a rising generation, they must learn to reflect on their practice, and to do so in the widest possible terms in order to embrace all its implications.
>
> (Kelly, 1995: 136)

4

STUDENT TEACHER
DEVELOPMENT

By the end of the decade, the government had introduced a
training system which in both structure and content reflected
its ideology: its orientation was 'practical', theory was disap-
pearing, increased responsibility had been given to teachers and
tutors had been portrayed as inadequate professionals.

(Wilkin, 1996: 168)

INTRODUCTION

In the late 1980s, the development of a National Curriculum for
schools brought with it the term 'delivery'. The use of this term in
educational contexts was resisted by many teachers and teacher educators for years, but it is now ubiquitous. Elliot Eisner (1982: 6)
reminds us that the metaphors we use 'shape our conception of the
problems we study'. A curriculum which is to be *delivered* does not
imply the need for a thinking teacher who is developing critical
thinking in his/her pupils. Rather, the teacher is required to be little
more than an educational Postman Pat *delivering* packages of
curriculum content. Such a model of the teacher, of course, has ramifications for the type of NQT to be developed by HEIs. Chapter 1
showed how much of the driving force for the government's changes
to teacher education in the 1980s came from writers associated with
the New Right, such as O'Hear (1988), the Hillgate Group (1989)
and Lawlor (1990). Student teachers, it was argued, needed to be
taught *what* to teach rather than *how* to teach (Lawlor, 1990). With
a 'sound knowledge and a love of the subject' (O'Hear, 1988):

Students would be sent into the classroom to learn to teach
as an essential part of their training. The individual qualities

67

of the teacher would be developed as he taught his subject. He would develop the characteristics of the good teacher in the classroom, use his common sense and acquire confidence, rather than be taught generalised theories irrelevant to good teaching.

(Lawlor, 1990: 21)

Subsequently, Circular 9/92 heralded the era of competence-based teacher education with a requirement for substantial elements of courses to be based in school. In the case of PGCE secondary programmes, this requirement was stipulated to be for 24 of the 36 weeks available, a model which appears to agree with the proposal that 'apprenticeship should take precedence over instruction and even when formal instruction is necessary it can never substitute for real practical training' (Hillgate Group, 1989: 9). No longer would there be a perceived theory–practice divide, because theoretical approaches to teaching would not exist. The teacher-as-technician would deliver the National Curriculum having been trained under apprenticeship, or competence-based, models of teacher development.

Language

The language that surrounds and defines the practices and processes of teacher education is an example of 'communication in an insti-tutionalised socio-cultural context' (Bhatia, 1993: 4). Since the inception of courses which comply with DES Circular 9/92, the term 'competence' has become central to the language of teacher education; so, too, has terminology of widely differing meaning, such as 'apprenticeship' and 'reflective practice'. On the one hand, teacher development is characterised as the acquisition of skills and content, while on the other hand, as we shall show later in this chapter, it is argued that teacher development is concerned with developing the processes of critical thinking in reflective practitioners. It is common to find in official documents and texts on teacher development the terms 'teacher education' and 'teacher training' used as if they are interchangeable. However, *education* and *training* are two very different processes, each of which might imply the user's underlying conception of teacher development. The establishment of a Teacher Training Agency (TTA) rather than a Teacher Education Agency perhaps has more to do with beliefs about the nature of teaching and how that 'craft' might best be learned, rather than a concern about acronyms.

After the introduction of secondary PGCE courses based upon Circular 9/92, it was clear that there would be major developments in the work undertaken by teachers in school engaged in supporting the development of student teachers. Similarly, there would be changes in the work of the HEI tutor, who had been, perhaps, hitherto characterised, not to say parodied, as the 'teaching practice supervisor' – the sometimes enigmatic, ghost-like figure, who would flit into and out of school and who would on occasions haunt the back of a student's classroom. The major assessment of the student's quality would be left to the teaching practice supervisor. However, Circular 9/92, with its espousal of 'competence', and the requirement that a large proportion of student teacher time be spent in school, meant that as well as the HEI tutor developing new ways of working, the classroom teacher would also need to develop the knowledge, understandings and skills required for the new role as a 'partner'. Subsequently, changes in terminology in HEI course documentation such as those from 'teaching practice' to 'school experience' and 'teaching practice school' to 'partnership school' reflect the change in philosophy and pedagogy of ITE courses.

The importance of the language that defines the practices and processes of teacher education lies in the fact that 'A particular set of discourse practices and conventions may achieve a high degree of *naturalisation* – they may come to be seen as simply "there" in a common-sense way, rather than socially put there' (Fairclough, 1992: 9). As shown in Chapter 3, much official documentation and the writings of the New Right attempt naturalisation of the teacher education discourse by characterising teaching as a value-free, practical craft – the values which underpin recent proposals are presented as 'common sense'.

STUDENT TEACHER DEVELOPMENT

In the quotation above, Lawlor argues that teachers can best learn their craft by applying 'common sense' to experience. The term 'common sense' here is seen as unproblematic. It presupposes that everyone knows what a 'good' teacher is, what is 'good' teaching and so on. Such a view, of course, fundamentally deprofessionalises not only the HEI tutor but the school teacher, too. It also exemplifies the belief that all can make statements about teaching which are equally valid, because everyone has been to school and everyone has 'common sense'. Such a belief has gained so much ground that 'in recent years, "theory" has been in danger of becoming a dirty word in relation to teacher education' (McIntyre, 1993: 39). The 'common sense' case has been made, and in the latter half of the 1990s it continues to be made, against the theoretical foundations of teacher education courses:

> School experience has turned out to be far from practical. It is seen as an opportunity to put theory into practice . . . general theory continues to dominate at the expense of individual practice; and students are not encouraged to approach classroom teaching with an open mind, or to develop individually as teachers. Instead they are expected to apply to their teaching, the generalised educational theories which they have been taught.
>
> (Lawlor, 1990: 21)

Again, this quotation shows the dichotomy of beliefs about the nature of teacher development: the development of the skilled craftsman or woman is opposed to the development of the critical thinker. Despite Circular 9/92's emphasis on the practical, despite inspections by HMI which showed that the circular has been implemented, despite HMCI's proposals for almost immediate reinspection of HEIs in 1996, it is still believed that there is too much theory forced upon student teachers. The proposed introduction of a National Curriculum for teacher training would appear to confirm a desire to reduce the theoretical content of ITE programmes. However, the Modes of Teacher Education (MOTE) research project's report *Partnership in Initial Teacher Education: A Topography* (Whiting et al., 1996) demonstrates clearly that many of the 'orthodoxies that government and media commentators often associate with HEI provision were rarely in evidence' in their findings. Less than 10 per cent of the institutions surveyed described the kind of teacher they aimed to produce as 'theoretically informed' (Whiting et al., 1996).

THEORISING AND REFLECTION

Lawlor is wrong in her interpretation of the word 'theory' as if it is either impractical intellectualism or some kind of educational dogma fed to student teachers to enact mechanically. If we return to the root of the word, the Greek *theoria*, we find it means *to look, to observe, to reflect*. Theory, now often defined and presented as 'theorising' in teacher education courses (Alexander, 1986), is in essence very practical. During the last ten years 'notions of "theorising", "theory as process" or "reflecting" have largely displaced the teaching of theory as propositional knowledge' in the majority of teacher education programmes (Furlong and Maynard, 1995: 38).

> I would argue, the theoretical knowledge which we offer student teachers should be treated by them as tentative, inadequate and constantly to be questioned and where appropriate, falsified; but it should also be knowledge which we offer to them because we believe it to be of practical value to them as teachers. Our commitment to the process of experimentation and falsification should be equalled by our commitment to making available to our students theoretical knowledge which they will, mostly, with refinement, be able usefully to assimilate to their professional thinking.
>
> (McIntyre, 1993: 41)

In recent years, the terms 'reflection' and 'the reflective practitioner' (Schön, 1983; Calderhead, 1989; Lucas, 1991; Rudduck, 1991) have become central to ITE programmes run by HEIs. Indeed, it would appear that the reflective practitioner is now 'the dominant model of professional in teacher education' (Whiting et al., 1996). It has been argued that the development of a reflective framework in teacher education was a response to the criticisms of the New Right, which sought to reduce teaching to an unproblematic, value-free, practical activity and that it was an attempt to re-intellectualise the teaching profession (Quicke, 1996). As many have observed (see, for example, Zeichner, 1983; Calderhead, 1989; Tabachnick and Zeichner, 1991; Hartley, 1993; Quicke, 1996), 'a number of competing models and conceptions of the "reflective practitioner" exist, varying in the meaning which they give to the terminology they use and in the nature of the theoretical articulation of the notion which they offer' (McLaughlin, 1996: 3). Zeichner (1994: 18) has called for more rigour in defining 'reflection': in order to further our understandings of teacher development, 'We need to focus our attention on what kind of reflection teachers are engaging in, on what it is teachers are reflecting about, and on how they are going about it.'

Calderhead (1989) provides a useful overview of the definitions of 'reflection' which have emerged in the writing related to teaching and teacher education. To varying degrees, reflective practice is seen to incorporate, *inter alia*, a variety of features including: problem

71

setting and solving; the development of analytical skills and attitudes which facilitate reflection, such as self-awareness and self-determination; the examination of values, moral principles and ideological and institutional constraints. Such features encompass, and are the foundation of, the *process, content, preconditions* and *product* of reflection. Korthagen and Wubbels (1995: 55) sum up reflection as 'the mental process of structuring or restructuring an experience, a problem or existing knowledge or insights'.

There is not scope in this chapter fully to explore the nature and scope of reflection, but McLaughlin (1996: 6–13) usefully locates conceptions of reflection along two continua. The first continuum refers to the *nature* of reflection. At one end are versions of reflection which stress the 'explicit and systematic' (cf. Dewey, 1933); at the other end, the 'implicit and intuitive' (Schön, 1987). The second continuum concerns itself with the *scope* and *objects* of reflection:

> One way of describing the continuum on which the scope and objects of reflection are located is in terms of a concern at one end of the continuum for specific and proximate matters and a concern at the other for matters which are general and contextual.
>
> (McLaughlin, 1996: 12)

McIntyre (1993) identifies three levels of reflection which are embedded in the Oxford Internship scheme: the *technical* level – concerned with the attainment of goals; the *practical* level – concerned with the 'assumptions, predispositions, values and consequences with which actions are linked'; and the *critical* or *emancipatory* level, where concern ranges to wider social, political and ethical issues, which include 'the institutional and societal forces which may constrain the individual's freedom of action or limit the efficacy of his or her actions' (McIntyre, 1993: 44). Such structuring draws on Carr and Kemmis' (1986) work with categories derived from Habermas (1974). While such categorisation may help to clarify thinking about reflection in an attempt to articulate teacher development, there is the danger that the implied hierarchy of these three levels can lead us to believe that reflection at the *practical* level is inferior to *critical* reflection (see Griffiths and Tann, 1992).

If we accept that different levels of reflection can be identified, we must also acknowledge that student teachers will engage in reflection in different ways, at different times, for different reasons. Frost

(1993: 140) helpfully summarises the *purposes* of reflection and how the process enables the student teacher to:

- assess his or her own skills and to improve them;
- evaluate the chosen teaching strategies and materials in terms of their appropriateness;
- question the values embedded in those practices and proceed to challenge the aims and goals for teacher education;
- continue to examine and clarify his or her personal values and beliefs about society and pedagogy;
- theorise about the context of his or her pedagogical practice – that is, to try to develop explanations about the pupils, the interactions in the classroom and about the processes of teaching and learning;
- examine the adequacy of theories about pedagogical contexts and processes and develop a critique of them.

Clearly, then, the case has been made that teacher development is a process which is more complex than a simple apprenticeship and that reflection within an ITE course enables a student teacher to develop practice in the short term, and also begins the development of habitual reflection that subsequently enables the teacher to continue to improve practice throughout his or her career. To elaborate: structured, guided reflection on, or analysis of, a student teacher's own practice, in the light of required reading, or school-based investigations which are part of an ITE course, will begin to develop initial competence in the context of a particular school-experience classroom. This experience will also develop practices of reflection which NQTs may use in whatever school context they find themselves subsequently, and which they may continue to use during their careers to facilitate their professional development. If such practices are believed to be beneficial, can they also be defended in relation to knowledge of student teacher development?

MODELS OF DEVELOPMENT

Circular 9/92 has required all secondary courses to focus on competences throughout the period of ITT. It is clear, however, that the term 'competence' has been interpreted, or constructed, in many different ways. Jones and Moore (1993) have offered a critique of competences which indicates how the State can extend its control over the sphere of professional expertise. They claim that competences can be altered to redefine the professional task of management or to hold professionals accountable through audit measures. Professionals are seen as technicians who are trained to operate a structure created by someone else, so there is no question of their defining and policing their own practices. Stromach *et al.* (1994) describe three types of competence for teacher education: 'coping competences', 'vernacular competences' and 'realised competences'. First, coping competence is displayed when the student teacher learns to fit in, to deal with confrontation, to negotiate an acceptable identity with pupils and teachers and to establish an acceptable reputation in the school. Second, vernacular competence is achieved through trial and error and is either a temporary or a permanent feature of a developing 'style' and 'persona' supported by the advice of teachers. This second stage has a great deal to do with developing viable working relationships rather than a concern with learning outcomes. Third, realised competence is observed when relationships are more stable and discipline issues recede in importance for the student teacher. It is at this stage that there is an emergence of firmer beliefs about pupil learning and the nature of teaching.

As described in Chapter 1, a further criticism of Circular 9/92's version of competence is the complete absence of an attempt to define exactly both the 'contexts' and 'levels of proficiency' required of newly qualified teachers' competences. Similarly, the central criticism of the Northern Ireland Working Group I (DENI, 1993a) on competence is that behavioural competences are at best mechanistic and take 'little account of the fact that in real life a competence can only be applied in specific contexts' (par. 6). Further, the working group insisted on the need to view competences as 'developmental' rather than 'minimum thresholds' (par. 18). Some courses, according to Whiting *et al.* (1996), have been using threshold competences (achieved/not yet achieved) and others favoured developmental competences (rating different kinds of development).

However, the Northern Ireland model of competence development is, perhaps, the most sophisticated and far-reaching as it relates development to three co-ordinated stages of teacher education: Stage I: Initial Teacher Training; Stage II: Induction; Stage III: The Further Professional Development of Teachers (DENI, 1993a: 6–15). Such a model acknowledges that development of competence goes far beyond the period of ITE. Furthermore, the 'weighting' of competences indicates which competences were most likely to be developed

during which stage of a teacher's career. The development of 'understanding of the arguments in favour of a balanced and broa based curriculum', for example, is appropriate to Stage I and m be achieved with little or no school experience; whereas 'takes appr priate responsibility for curriculum leadership' is more likely to b appropriate to Stages II or III. A full list of the Northern Irelan competences may be found in Appendix A.

However, despite a variety of interpretations of the term 'compe-tence' in relation to student teacher development:

> As yet we have very little detailed understanding of how stud-ents develop their own practical professional knowledge in relation to such competences; how they combine their prac-tical experience and other forms of learning in order to develop skills, knowledge and understandings necessary to be compe-tent practitioners.
>
> (Furlong and Maynard, 1995: vii)

Although there is but a small, if growing, body of knowledge about the ways in which student teachers learn to become teachers, Berliner (1994) claims to be able to identify clear stages in the development of teacher expertise. Drawing upon similarities exhibited by experts in a range of areas including chess, nursing, football, air-traffic control and racehorse handicapping, Berliner proposes five stages through which the teacher journeys:

> We begin with the greenhorn, the raw recruit, the *novice*. Student teachers and many first-year teachers may be consid-ered novices. As experience is gained, the novice becomes an *advanced beginner*. Many second- and third-year teachers are likely to be in this developmental stage. With further experi-ence and some motivation to succeed, the advanced beginner becomes a *competent* performer. It is likely that many third- and fourth-year teachers, as well as some more experienced teachers, are at this level. At about the fifth year, a modest number of teachers may move into the *proficient* stage. Finally, a small number of these will move on to the last stage of devel-opment – that of *expert* teacher.
>
> (Berliner, 1994: 108)

While Berliner admits that the developmental sequence involved in the progression from novice to expert 'is not as yet clearly described' and that his proposition is presented to promote thought

about teacher development, his model seems highly questionable for a number of reasons. The attempt to equate 'expert' nurses and teachers with racehorse handicappers and footballers seems tenuous in the extreme. Perhaps the most significant area for debate, given the current practice of competence-based teacher education, is Berliner's belief that *competent* teaching, which is characterised by teachers' ability to 'make conscious decisions about what they are going to do' and the ability to 'know what to attend to and what to ignore', is achieved only after at least three or four years of teaching. Is he suggesting that, prior to this stage, teachers are *incompetent*? Circular 9/92 expects competence of NQTs. Berliner's model also raises the question that if only 'a modest number of teachers' will ever become *proficient*, how many can possibly have the experience and qualities necessary to mentor? Clearly, the model of development is flawed when applied to teaching.

Berliner's description of the novice also seems overly simplistic. It ignores not only the diversity of entrants to teacher education courses, but also the range of knowledge, experience and expertise they bring with them (see, for example, Calderhead and Robson, 1991). Entrants to PGCE courses may be the newly graduated 21-year-olds; but, equally, the PGCE student teacher may be the Ph.D. research chemist with twenty years' work experience in industry; the single parent in his early thirties with a master's degree; the Benedictine brother; the EFL teacher who has spent twenty-five years teaching in Europe and the Middle East; the mother of grown-up children returning to teaching; the priest, and anyone with any other experience. While such student teachers might not have the characteristics of one of Berliner's *expert* teachers, all bring diverse knowledge, experience and expertise. As Furlong and Maynard (1995: 182) observe, it is 'important to recognise that no student teacher enters the classroom as a complete novice – they bring with them a vast array of skills, knowledge and understandings derived from other contexts'. We will return to this discussion later in the chapter.

STAGES OF DEVELOPMENT

Calderhead's research identifies three phases through which student teachers pass. These phases, 'fitting in', 'passing the test' and 'exploring' (Calderhead, 1987: 269–278), appear to confirm the findings of the much earlier work of Fuller and Bown (1975). More recently, the research conducted by Furlong and Maynard (1995)

has done much in attempting to exemplify contemporary student teacher development in the primary school context. They propose five broad stages of development which student teachers undergo during school experience. They perceive each stage as having a complex set of characteristics and needs which call for mentors to prioritise certain kinds of activities. These stages are: 'early idealism', 'personal survival', 'dealing with difficulties', 'hitting a plateau' and 'moving on'. Furlong and Maynard are emphatic that these stages are not 'discrete or fixed; rather, they are . . . interrelated and mutable' (Furlong and Maynard, 1995: 73). Similarly, the writers are keen to stress that progression through these stages should not be viewed in a 'crude or simplistic way':

> We do not suggest that student teachers simply progress along a narrow linear pathway, moving smoothly from stage to stage. This is far from the case. Our research indicates that development from 'novice' to 'professional educator' is dependent on the interaction between individual students, their teacher education programme, and the school context in which they undertake practical experience. As a result, a student's learning is complex, erratic and in one sense unique to them as an individual.
>
> (Furlong and Maynard, 1995: 70)

What is particularly valuable in Furlong and Maynard's work is the recognition of the complexity and individuality of student teacher development.

Student teacher development can be seen to be the product of, among other things, the complex interactions between the individual, the HEI programme and the school context. Perhaps a useful analogy for the process is to think of student teacher development as taking place in the same way that a photographer develops a photograph in a developing tray. The image does not develop uniformly from nothing: at one moment a blank sheet; the next a fully formed, crystal-clear picture. Instead, as the image swims into view, different parts of it emerge simultaneously and independently: a highlight here; a fragment of landscape there; a detail of shadow; now a facial feature, until the complete image emerges. What emerges first and last depends on interactions between information stored in the paper and the chemicals acting upon it. Similarly, the development of the student teacher's practice, knowledge, understandings and beliefs is

77

a *synthesis of experiences*. In the classroom context it may be some time before a 'complete' picture emerges. Indeed, it may take many years. However, the process of synthesising enables the student teacher to focus, probe, test and begin to make sense of emerging classroom images. Information which the student teacher uses in this process may come from two main sources. The first source may be direct experience through observation or teaching in the classroom, while the second source may be a result of reading, writing or discussion with mentor, tutor, student teacher, other teachers or pupils, for example. Or, indeed, it is more likely that the student teacher will draw from a combination of both sources. In Chapter 7 we propose that this synthesis of experience is best facilitated through the student teacher's engagement in a dialogue of educational discourses. Clearly, there are implications for the subject mentor, who is likely to be most called upon by the student teacher during the early days of school experience, in which the development of this dialogue is critical.

Student teacher idealism

The complexities of student teacher development and the types of support which subject mentors might offer are discussed at length in Chapters 5, 6 and 7. It is useful, however, in this chapter to consider in some detail what has been said about the point at which student teachers begin their development.

The notion that the first perceptions of student teachers are simplistic or naive is commonplace (for example, McIntyre *et al.*, 1993: 97; Smith and Alred, 1993: 108; Elliott and Calderhead, 1993: 169). Furlong and Maynard describe the first stage of student teacher development as 'early idealism': it is a stage in which idealism is represented by student teachers' simplistic views of teaching and learning, and the expectation that they will be able to build friendly relationships with pupils, which they link with memories either of effective teachers who were able to do this, or ineffective teachers who were not. The work of Furlong and Maynard provides teacher educators (tutors and mentors) with useful points of departure for further research into student teacher development.

At the beginning of many secondary PGCE courses student teachers are asked to give their reasons for coming into teaching and to describe the 'skills, qualities and attributes of a good teacher'. The majority write about: 'enthusiasm', 'empathy', 'love of subject', 'the desire to share the love of subject'. The following examples were written by student teachers within the first week of a secondary PGCE course: 'My main reason for teaching stems from my love of the subject I wish to teach'; 'I hope my enthusiasm for maths can be passed on as part of my teaching'; 'If I can inspire pupils to be amazed by what a fantastic world they are part of, to enjoy their lives no matter what they are or become, then I might start considering myself as a teacher'; 'I am looking forward to being able to pass on my love and enthusiasm for my subject'; 'I think perhaps the most important attributes are enthusiasm and energy. These qualities are needed to inspire pupils and get them all involved'; 'I want to be the kind of teacher who can communicate my love of music to a class and instil in them a love of the subject'.

The focus on National Curriculum subjects in the student teachers' comments quoted, and in many others like them, is, without doubt, a corollary of the subject-based nature of secondary schooling. However, unlike the primary student teachers who were the main focus of Furlong and Maynard's research, secondary student teachers at this stage appear to place far less emphasis on the 'warm, friendly, caring' aspects of teaching associated with child-centred primary education (Furlong and Maynard, 1995: 74). Further, the feeling of 'vulnerability' described by Furlong and Maynard, induced in student teachers who were aware that class teachers saw their classrooms (and by implication their pupils) as their 'domain' (Furlong and Maynard, 1995: 77), has not emerged as an important issue with secondary student teachers in our study (see Chapter 5). The organisation of secondary schools, in which teachers will see perhaps four or five subject classes in a day, possibly in different classrooms, may mitigate against the development of a proprietorial air which primary student teachers may feel they detect in the primary school context. Importantly, Furlong and Maynard acknowledge the centrality of contextual factors in their findings, which they recognise must include the HEI programme and the schools in which student teachers are placed (Furlong and Maynard, 1995: 70). Moreover, our experience appears to confirm Furlong and Maynard's assertion of the importance of context, as it suggests that there are discernible and definite differences in student teacher concerns and anxieties at the beginning of a course, which are a result of the *phase* of education in which they are preparing to teach.

If we accept that the first stage of teacher development is characterised by 'early idealism', it is nevertheless important for us to clarify
what this term means, as 'idealism' has a number of meanings which
are both positive and negative. The word can mean: *love for, or search
after, the best; impracticality*, and *the imaginative treatment of subjects*.
Clearly, *idealism* may be equated with *impracticality*. However, in
our view, early idealism is linked much more positively, first, to the
important personal and potentially professional values student
teachers bring to ITE, and, second, as we attempt to show in Chapter
6, to ideas which are as complex as Furlong and Maynard suggest,
or even more sophisticated.

As Chapter 3 indicates, we emphasise the centrality of the student
teachers' own beliefs and values, which permeate their professional
development not only during the period of qualifying as teachers,
but also as NQTs and experienced teachers. Likewise, we fully
endorse Northern Ireland's assertion of the importance of the
'personal qualities' and 'professional attitudes' which enable the
student teacher to unify and synthesise knowledge, understandings
and experience gained in the classroom and 'to pull the individual
competences together and apply them in the professional context'
(DENI, 1993a: 4). Such qualities and attitudes should not be seen
simplistically as a kind of 'virtuous glue' which sticks together the
fragments of practice. Rather, such professional characteristics are
at the *core* of the student teacher's development and permeate the
development of professional knowledge and professional skills.
While such characteristics are 'general (and perhaps ideal)' (DENI,
1993a: 4), we believe that these permeating characteristics are not
fixed, but are equally developmental in their nature. We agree with
Furlong and Maynard that student teacher development does
not take place 'along a narrow linear pathway' of the sort that the
model of progression from 'novice' to 'expert' may suggest, but rather,
like the way in which a tree grows, teacher development has at
its core those values, beliefs and qualities both personal and professional which, perhaps, brought the student teacher to teaching in
the first instance, and which, with growth and development, may
sustain the teacher through his or her entire professional career.

CONCLUSION

As Chapter 1 demonstrated, since the inception of courses constructed in response to Circular 9/92, student teachers have learned

to teach within competence-based models of development. One of our criticisms of such a model of student teacher development is that implicit in it is an undue emphasis on teacher development as an *individual* journey. While individual student teacher development may be unique, the model pays insufficient attention to the social dynamics of becoming a teacher. It appears to undervalue the *process* of developing a personal philosophy which can be articulated and translated into practice through the synthesis of experiences.

Clearly, student teachers in the early stages of school experience may have difficulties in breaking down classroom practice in a way that enables them to begin to make sense of what is happening and how it is happening. 'Student teachers also appear to lack the analytical skills to examine their own practice – they lack a language for talking about teaching' (Calderhead, 1989: 46). While Calderhead's assertion that student teachers lack the 'analytical skills' to examine practice should be contested, it is true that they may initially lack the *tool* – language – which enables them so to do. It is here, in the early stages, when a student teacher is attempting to make sense of basic classroom practice, that indicators of competence, or statements describing competence, may be of use. They should be used neither as a tick list of skills or behaviours to adopt, nor as a simple checklist for the student teacher, subject mentor, or tutor against which to assess progress, but as a means of enabling student teachers to get inside the 'language' of teaching.

Teaching itself is like a language. It is not a language, but it has many similarities to one. Essentially, teaching is concerned with communication – of knowledge, of ideas, of facts or, indeed, beliefs. At one end of the continuum, it may be purely transactional, dealing with the transmission of content. Elsewhere, it may be entertaining, thought-provoking, challenging and even, at times, inspirational. In this sense we see statements of competence to be of most use as a *metalanguage* which enables tutor, mentor and student teacher to have a shared vocabulary with which to articulate the complexities of teaching. Such use of competence statements can enable the student teacher more quickly to focus and begin to see classrooms conceptually. When working with student teachers in school in the early stages, subject mentors, therefore, might more usefully view competence as part of the *process* of learning to teach rather than solely as a description of the *product* of a teacher education programme.

81

On many PGCE secondary courses, in the early stages of school experience, student teachers carry out systematic enquiry into aspects of teaching related to their own practice. The exact focuses may be chosen by student teachers, usually in discussion with tutors and/or mentors, in order to meet perceived needs, or to make visible some aspect of practice. Calderhead has criticised student teachers' ability to reflect, describing it as 'shallow' (Calderhead, 1987: 277). Certainly, the work student teachers produce early in their PGCE courses tends to be *descriptive* in nature rather than *reflective*. However, we believe that this fact should not surprise us, nor does it invalidate the activity, for it is in the initial stages, in such *articulation* or *description* of some aspect of practice which may seem blindingly obvious to the experienced teacher, that learning and development take place. Such description in these early stages can for the first time make visible the processes of teaching which are often otherwise concealed from observers by the experienced teacher's apparently seamless art.

Similarly, this articulation or description can allow student teachers to begin to probe their own personal theories of teaching and learning: the theories and images of teaching and learning which they bring to the teacher education course (Calderhead, 1992), described earlier in our discussion of 'idealism'. We agree with Griffiths and Tann (1992), who propose that we should not view reflection as hierarchical, privileging so-called *critical* reflection over *practical* reflection (McIntyre, 1993). In fact, student teachers, and experienced teachers too, need to engage in the forms of reflective practice which are most appropriate to particular contexts. In such a manner 'small-scale and particular' *personal* theories, which some might characterise as 'common sense', may be tested against and informed by 'large-scale and universal' *public* theories:

> Everyone has to start somewhere, and no-one can start everywhere. It is being argued that all of the levels are an essential part of reflective practice. At any one time the focus may be on one or another of them, but it is vital that each reflective practitioner should follow all of them at some time.
>
> (Griffiths and Tann, 1992: 79)

Subject mentors and tutors can enable student teachers to develop professionally: by engaging with their articulation of personal experience; by making visible the educational discourses embedded in their descriptions of experience and practice; and by engaging in dialogue which explores the contexts in which they are working in order to develop professionally.

Part II

DISCURSIVE SUBJECT MENTORING

5

TENDENCIES IN SUBJECT MENTORING

INTRODUCTION

The remaining chapters of this book are concerned with the development of practice in subject mentoring. Chapter 5 identifies significant tendencies in subject mentoring from research evidence of mentors' practice in supporting lesson planning, teaching and evaluation. It uses this evidence to argue a case for the practice of discursive subject mentoring. Chapter 6 identifies the field of educational discourses in which discursive subject mentoring takes place, and suggests that reference to this field of discourses can make subject mentoring more effective. Chapter 7 uses further research evidence and a case study to demonstrate how discursive mentoring can be practised in relation to collaborative teaching, making reference to the dialogue of educational discourses which is the context of teaching. In conclusion, Chapter 8 argues that the practice of discursive mentoring is best conducted within what may be called mentoring departments in mentoring schools. The argument of these chapters makes use of evidence from a study of subject mentors involved in a number of PGCE programmes between 1993 and 1996.

THE AIMS OF OUR STUDY

After the introduction of secondary PGCE courses based upon Circular 9/92, it was clear that there would need to be major changes in the working practices of tutors in HEIs and teachers in school engaged in supporting the development of student teachers. Both would need to develop the knowledge, understandings and skills required for the developing 'partnership' model of teacher education.

While we recognise the importance of the significant and complementary part played by the HEI tutor and acknowledge that the structure and quality of the university and college component of any PGCE course are of equal significance to the school-based element in the development of the student teacher, the main aim of the study was to explore the contribution which might be made by mentors.

The years 1992–1996 saw a rapid expansion in the literature which mapped the developing field of mentoring: for example, the works of Glover and Mardle (1995); Hagger *et al.* (1993); Kerry and Shelton Mayes (1995); Furlong and Maynard (1995); Stephens (1996); Tomlinson (1995b); Watkins and Whalley (1993); Wilkin (1992), to cite but a few. Given the emergent nature of the concept of mentoring in schools, it is unsurprising that, with a few exceptions, many texts focused in the main upon management issues, practices in mentoring, and considered how mentors might contribute to student teacher development. What was less evident was an account of the underlying processes which might help them to make such a contribution, particularly in the work of what has come to be called the subject mentor. Many texts during the early 1990s concentrated upon generic mentoring issues, rather than considering the subject-specific dimension of mentoring. Therefore, in 1993 we began our study, which involved both theoretical and empirical investigations. Initially, the authors wished to uncover what it was that mentors were doing with student teachers; how they were going about these activities; what was their rationale, and what, if any, were the perceived benefits to mentors, student teachers and pupils of mentoring practices described in the literature, such as 'collaborative teaching'.

Our research methodology, in the main, may be characterised as qualitative, not because of any polarity of views concerning the merits of qualitative and quantitative methodology, but because of the 'newness' of the widespread enterprise of mentoring in schools. Because we wished to explore the practices and processes of mentoring, qualitative methodology appeared most appropriate. Such methodology would also allow us to define our focus progressively as the study continued and as areas of interest or concern emerged. A pilot study comprising observation, questionnaire and follow-up interviews was conducted with fifty mentors in the south-east of England during 1993. The results raised further questions, which we continued to explore through recourse to the growing body of literature and by carrying out a second round of observation, questionnaire and interviews during 1994. Our results were leading us towards an exploration of the specific contribution of subject mentoring in the secondary school. We therefore planned to widen our study of mentors of PGCE secondary student teachers in the south-east of England during 1995 and 1996. In order to contextualise our growing understandings we carried out two further studies in order to place our work in the larger context.

First, we conducted interviews of key personnel managing and teaching secondary teacher education courses in all areas of the United Kingdom in order to map the development of partnership-based courses and to explore emergent aspects of mentoring. Second, we drew on inspection evidence in England and interviewed HMI in Scotland and Northern Ireland to gain their perspectives on the developments of partnerships and mentoring in secondary PGCE courses throughout the UK.

Subsequently, during 1995–1996, a questionnaire was circulated to 200 subject mentors in 65 schools involved in a number of teacher education partnerships with HEIs. Subject mentors were invited to indicate their attitudes to a number of features of school-based, partnership PGCEs, and to describe their practices in contributing to them. These subject mentors had between one and three years' experience of working within partnership models of ITE. The 135 returned, completed questionnaires were analysed and follow-up interviews took place with a selection of subject mentors. Unattributed quotations in this part of the book are from mentors consulted in the research. We acknowledge, of course, that subject mentoring in schools is still in its infancy and understandings of the processes of mentoring are still growing and will continue to grow in coming years. Therefore, we present our work as a contribution to the discussion of mentoring in the hope that it will further the understanding of the processes of subject mentoring for mentor and tutor alike, and, perhaps, suggest further areas for research.

OBSERVING SUBJECT MENTORS TEACHING

As indicated above, this chapter is concerned with the identification of tendencies in subject mentoring. Its premise is that describing and defining how subject mentors work in practice is a necessary step towards determining what can be done to make subject mentoring as effective as possible. The chapter begins by identifying tendencies in subject mentoring which are manifested in the ways in which student teachers and subject mentors interact in the cycles of planning, teaching and evaluation which are central to school experience in ITE and, of course, to the working lives of teachers.

Subject mentors in our study considered classroom observation to be the single most effective developmental activity used in ITE. They considered their own lesson observations highly effective, and they wanted HEI tutors to devote more time to classroom observations because of the high value they placed upon them. They stressed the importance of communication between tutors and mentors about these observations, commenting favourably on their experiences of joint observation and 'triangular' follow-up discussions involving the mentor, tutor and student teacher, seeing these as one of the most important means by which the quality of ITE partnerships is developed. Subject mentors also considered student teacher observation of their own lessons a very effective developmental activity. However, comments showed that subject mentors hold a range of opinions about what makes these practices effective, and these ideas are suggestive of very different kinds of subject mentor/student teacher relationships and tendencies in subject-mentoring practice.

Access to planning and the benefits of observation

Subject mentors reported a number of methods by which student teachers gained access to their own planning processes. Some student teachers are invited to participate democratically at department planning meetings. One subject mentor wrote: 'All planning in our department is shared planning.' Other student teachers are presented with model lesson plans of the kind which subject mentors expect them to produce for their own lessons.

Most subject mentors indicated that it is important for student teachers' observations to have a focus, many stressing the value of opportunities to isolate particular aspects of classroom management such as timing or giving instructions. One subject mentor saw this kind of opportunity as a major benefit of school-based ITE: 'Focus on particular aspects of class management without having to learn by trial and error is a big step forward.' Some subject mentors, however, suggested that focuses should help student teachers to see that teachers make reference to a much wider range of considerations than classroom management in determining how and what to plan and teach: 'Student teachers need a clear understanding of what they are observing and for what purpose; e.g. one week it may be subject knowledge/content, another time it could be teaching styles, another classroom management.'

A similar range of views was indicated in subject mentors' comments on the value of student teachers observing their lessons. Some saw this as an opportunity for them to glean information that would help with classroom management: 'Student teachers who observe classes they will teach later on can get to know the names and character of pupils, giving them a head start.' Others, however, concentrated on the ways in which observation of the subject mentor can help to develop a professional relationship in which mentor and student teacher share experiences, and are consequently able to be open with each other in discussion, one noting, 'It reminds subject mentors of the pressures observation can induce.'

These responses suggest that subject mentors hold different views about the ways in which student teachers should acquire knowledge, ranging from those who see them as apprentices who learn by copying skills, to those who see them as co-enquirers and developers of effective practice, whose reflective thinking needs to take account of numerous considerations.

Debriefing

Subject mentors were asked about the value of deconstructing their own practice after they had been observed in the classroom. They indicated wide variations in the extent to which they valued and adopted this practice, ranging from those who found it self-evident that it is necessary ('Obviously you discuss/analyse the lesson critically – don't you always!') to those who simply stated that they had never attempted it. The exclamation mark completing the comment of the subject mentor quoted suggests a real commitment to reflective practice which student teachers would be encouraged to emulate. It is difficult to imagine how subject mentors who do not reflect on their own practice with student teachers can convincingly argue that reflection is part of the working lives of real teachers.

Of those subject mentors who do deconstruct their practice, some were extremely confident and had well-established routines, such as providing student teachers with a written self-evaluation after the lesson. 'I enjoy this. It is important to be able to explain what we are doing and why – if we can't do this then we are little more than shamans who claim power but don't know where it comes from!' Others who had tried, indicated that they did not have a vocabulary to deconstruct practice in any useful way: 'It can be quite difficult to be analytical of your own teaching methods without saying "It will happen with experience."' Interestingly, those subject mentors who were most confident about deconstructing practice often made comments which showed that they were able to see lessons as having adopted one of a range of possible strategies, or that they were able to move comfortably from practical to theoretical considerations in their analysis. One subject mentor called deconstruction 'an excellent focusing exercise which helps "demystify" the seemingly easy flow of a lesson, making it easier to explain why certain strategies were chosen and why others may not work'.

The words 'shaman' and 'demystify' are typical of the language used by a number of subject mentors, who implied that their role is to pass on the esoteric secrets of the professional teacher. Others, however, presented the practice of lesson deconstruction as one in which the student teacher was challenged to take the lead in discussing the subject mentor's work, using the same analytical skills which the subject mentor would apply when observing him or her: deconstruction was described by one subject mentor as taking place when 'meeting to review practice and how the student teacher could contribute to developing the subject mentor'. Another subject mentor who sought to promote this kind of dialogue commented on the significance of the dynamics of the relationship between subject mentor and student teacher: 'I find it immensely valuable to discuss my lessons and evaluate them with student teachers. They often find it somewhat embarrassing because they feel unable to make critical observations or suggest ways they might have tackled a situation. This improves with time.' Clearly, this subject mentor works at creating real dialogue because of a belief in its importance in student teacher development.

Subject mentors ranged from those who saw debriefing as about the passing on of esoteric knowledge which is difficult to articulate, to those who held open discussions in which student teachers take an active role, analysing lessons with reference to a wide range of possible teaching strategies.

OBSERVING STUDENT TEACHERS' LESSONS

Access to planning

Subject mentors typically described discussing planning with student teachers at regular weekly meetings, many indicating that, whatever time allowance was made by the school or the partnership, more was needed. One subject mentor voiced the typical view of planning discussions as follows: 'It is vital at the beginning of a practice and should continue for as long as possible and certainly until the subject mentor is happy with the quality of planning and the quality of teaching . . . a top priority.'

However, the reasons given for the importance of the practice were, once again, very varied. It was often partly seen in terms of the subject mentor's and the school's ultimate responsibility to pupils, who cannot afford to have inappropriate teaching: 'Time has to be made available to ensure pupil continuity and that the student teacher's input is appropriate.' As in some of the comments made about the practice of observing subject mentors teach, there is an emphasis here on the value of forms of learning for student teachers which eliminate unnecessary mistakes. However, some subject mentors argued that planning discussions which covered, and made connections between, a range of educational considerations were the most valuable. For example, some Science subject mentors found it important to establish how the view of science a student teacher had derived from university experience related to National Curriculum requirements; some Modern Languages subject mentors wanted to ensure that a student teacher's use of the target language was based on an understanding of subject pedagogy.

Observation strategies

The establishment of a focus was regarded by most subject mentors as the key to effective lesson observation, especially in the early stages, when student teachers may otherwise be overwhelmed by the number of different considerations which are involved in teaching a lesson. Many subject mentors indicated that the focuses they choose or negotiate are normally defined in terms of areas of competence. However, as one put it: 'Although subject mentors should focus on pre-agreed areas, most student teachers also appreciate feedback on the whole lesson as well', and the value of recording methods which capture 'whatever happens that seems important' was indicated by several others. Once again subject mentors described a variety of approaches, which range from observations which are concerned with confirming the achievement of skills, to those which are concerned with drawing out how the decisions made and actions taken in the process of teaching relate in very complex ways to numerous educational considerations.

Debriefing

Subject mentors expressed a very wide range of views about what makes debriefing effective. The apparent capacity for reflection and professional objectivity of the student teachers they had worked with in the past was a crucial factor in determining these views. Thus, while some subject mentors indicated that 'student teachers find self-evaluation very difficult without a lot of guidance', others suggested that 'student teachers know, intuitively, in most cases, what was good and what was bad'. Similarly, whereas some subject mentors held the view that 'student teachers are so firm in their opinions that they find it very difficult to address their weaknesses', others argued that 'student teachers can sometimes be very hard on themselves'.

Those who found student teachers poor at self-evaluation stressed the importance of subject mentors taking the lead: 'Some sort of immediate feedback from the subject mentor is needed'; 'Some student teachers struggle to get to the main point so a check-off list is needed.' Those who found them more effective self-evaluators tended to encourage student teachers to begin the analysis in any debriefing, and saw their own role as deepening it: 'The subject mentor can explain weaknesses rather than highlighting them.' Subject mentors who considered student teachers poor at identifying weaknesses insisted on the importance of their own intervention to ensure that 'the student teacher knows where the weaknesses lie and has ideas/strategies for improving', but those who had found them over-critical tended to argue: 'It is very easy to see what goes wrong. But the focus for development must be on what went right. The student teachers thrive on praise.'

These differences suggest that subject mentors consider the student teacher's capacity for reflection a key factor in determining how useful dialogue is in debriefing. Of course, there is a real possibility that subject mentors who expect student teachers to be poor at evaluation create a self-fulfilling prophecy which is 'confirmed' when they dominate debriefing. However, a number of subject mentors drew attention to other factors which affect the possibility of making the debriefing process one which involves real dialogue. Time is very significant here: 'When there is insufficient time, student teacher opinion is cut short.' When time is short, subject mentors are more likely to impose an interpretation of a lesson on the student teacher, rather than allowing one to be collaboratively constructed.

PRAGMATIC AND DISCURSIVE TENDENCIES IN SUBJECT MENTORING

Despite their universal commendation of the effectiveness of lesson observation in developing student teachers, it is clear that the practice and expectations of the subject mentors who completed the research questionnaire are very different. There are some subject mentors whose practice focuses on the *pragmatic*, drawing attention most frequently to matters such as classroom management issues with immediate practical application; who indicate that they see their teaching role as transmitting knowledge about what practice works and what does not; and who describe their assessment function as monitoring the development of student teachers' skills or competences. At the opposite end of the spectrum there are subject mentors whose practice focuses on the *discursive*, who make reference to a wide range of educational considerations, often emphasising those which have subject-specific aspects; who see their teaching role as one of guiding collaborative enquiry into educational theory and practice; and who describe their assessment function as developing critical thinkers or reflective practitioners.

The responses of many subject mentors suggest that they operate a more pragmatic model of subject mentoring at the beginning of their work with student teachers and when supporting those whose development is slow, moving towards a more discursive model with time, and as student teachers progress. It is also true that time and other constraints, including the DfEE requirement for partnerships to adopt competence-based models of ITE, limit the extent to which subject mentors can adopt a discursive model, but the responses to the research questionnaire suggested that a subject mentor's implicit or explicit theories of classroom teaching and of teacher development are just as significant determinants of subject mentoring practice.

Table 1 Pragmatic and discursive tendencies in subject mentoring

Mentoring feature	Mentors working pragmatically tend to:	Mentors working discursively tend to:
Subject mentor training and meetings	believe that initial mentor training on procedures was adequate; prefer meeting agendas limited to course procedures;	perceive opportunities to share mentor experiences as training; want to use meetings to explore subject teaching issues;
Communication	welcome partnership communications in the form of brief reminders about procedures;	value partnership communications which address current subject teaching issues, and seek to contribute to them;
Liaison with subject tutors	consider the subject tutor role in school to be to check student teacher assessment;	expect subject tutors to be involved in collaborative activities in school; want to contribute to HE teaching sessions;
Student teacher support	present student teachers with documents such as schemes of work and then expect them to take initiative in seeking further advice;	initiate discussion of the principles informing department documentation made available to student teachers;
Lesson observation and debriefing	prefer competence-based proformas for lesson observation; initiate the discussion in lesson debriefings;	prefer open-ended and timeline approaches to lesson observation; encourage student teachers to initiate discussion in debriefings;
Prioritisation of educational discourses	place emphasis on classroom management skills in discussions with student teachers;	place emphasis on pupil learning and subject teaching issues in discussions with student teachers;
Use of own teaching in mentoring	use their own lessons to model practice for student teachers to observe and emulate;	use their own lessons as a basis for dialogue about subject teaching which student teachers are expected to lead;
Collaborative teaching	move student teachers quickly towards independent 'solo' teaching;	make use of collaborative teaching throughout student teachers' school experience for the benefit of pupils and teachers;

Table 1 Continued

Mentoring feature	Mentors working pragmatically tend to:	Mentors working discursively tend to:
Contribution to student teachers' non-teaching work	believe student teachers' written assignments are 'college work' to be undertaken independently;	want to discuss the theoretical issues student teachers address in written assignments, and help find practical focuses;
Weak student teachers	expect the HEI to take quick, firm action on ' weak students', such as transferring them to another school;	negotiate and monitor informal targets with 'weak student teachers' before instigating formal procedures;
Subject knowledge	interpret subject knowledge mainly as the knowledge needed to teach the National Curriculum and/or school schemes of work.	regard subject knowledge as a multifaceted discourse, which student teachers can explore with department members.

Subject mentors in the study grouped their responses to a wide range of questions in ways which identified them as tending towards pragmatic or discursive subject mentoring practice. Table 1, 'Pragmatic and discursive tendencies in subject mentoring', indicates how these tendencies are represented in a particular set of subject mentoring attitudes and practices.

We suggest that it is possible to identify two broad types of subject mentoring which we characterise as *pragmatic* and *discursive*. The two types proposed are not, of course, rigid polarised forms of mentoring to which a subject mentor might cling. Rather they represent ends of a continuum along which mentoring practice might be located. Nor should a subject mentor's practice be regarded as necessarily fixed. It may indeed change to reflect the subject mentor's perceived level of development of the student teacher. However, the work of Williams *et al.* (1996) into the form, function and focus of mentor/student teacher dialogue found 'issues related to class management and subject application predominant'.

PRAGMATIC MENTORING

There are several reasons why subject mentors may tend to adopt pragmatic subject mentoring practices. First, teachers who were 'trained' before school-based ITE was introduced may have had limited support from schools and still survived. Teachers whose implicit or explicit learning theory is that 'you learn only by doing' may believe that the most important function of school experience is to anticipate the first year in post, and that, since this crucially involves facing and overcoming survival problems, making student teachers work independently is an important priority. Teachers may also believe that time for reflective practice and reading about 'theory' is not realistically available to teachers who experience the timetable loads and administrative pressures schools face in the 1990s, and that consequently, encouraging student teachers to make use of them teaches them to use crutches which will be suddenly removed, with disastrous consequences.

Other evidence from the study suggests that some student teachers like pragmatic subject mentoring. They relish the opportunity it gives them to 'stand on their own feet' and take on the challenges of a real teacher in their own classroom with the door shut. The sense of difficulty they feel in attempting to solve the problems that may arise on their own further demonstrates to them that they are 'doing it' like real teachers, who, they know, face 'difficulty' every day of their working lives. However, the limitations of pragmatic subject mentoring are apparent if we consider the likely impact of influential pragmatic subject mentors on student teachers. Their student teachers are likely to see 'theory' as a single undifferentiated block of ideas which has little classroom relevance, and written assignments which call for the consideration of theoretical perspectives as 'college work'. They are also likely to experience dialogue with subject mentors which so privileges classroom management that, once a degree of classroom control has been achieved, they will feel competent. It may also be the case that, while student teachers recognise the importance of teaching the National Curriculum, they are unable to make an effective critical interpretation of it through which decisions about practice can be justified. They are likely to perceive the support they receive as encouraging them to copy practice, to teach as they are told or what they have been shown.

DISCURSIVE MENTORING

Student teachers who are supported by discursive subject mentoring practices are likely to perceive their subject mentors as explorers of subject teaching issues, to value intellectual and practical activities which enable them to make connections between the discourse of their academic subject, subject teaching pedagogy, the subject curriculum and the classroom, and to believe that their PGCE course has given them access to many different theories and viewpoints. They are likely to perceive their experience of the course as successfully integrated. They are likely to see tutors and subject mentors as having overlapping, rather than discrete, expertise, and to consult either, about both classroom teaching and written assignments with a theoretical bias. They are likely to see any teaching strategy they adopt as one of a range available to them which may limit some possibilities in the classroom even while it opens up others. They are likely to question anything which is presented to them as certainty, to want to consult others and to investigate matters themselves. They are likely to develop the perspective of critical interpreters of the National Curriculum.

Discursive subject mentoring recognises the functions of dialogue in learning. The next two chapters will consider ways in which discursive subject mentoring can access the dialogue among different educational discourses which, it will be suggested, takes place in the thinking of reflective teachers. In particular, it will be argued that discursive subject mentoring can recognise and make extended reference to important subject-specific discourses. Discursive subject mentoring can also provide a means of encouraging student teachers to seek access to the more theoretical aspects of educational discourses, in a manner which is appropriate to school-based ITE. These features make discursive subject mentoring a significantly political activity. It can contribute to the education of teachers who will expect to be able to participate in the discourses through which the subject curriculum and the school curriculum are developed. It will encourage teachers to make connections between the postmodern definitions of meaning in the academic disciplines they have studied as undergraduates, which will have taken account of social, cultural and historical contexts, and meaning in the subject curriculum as it is defined in the National Curriculum. It will equip them to question the appropriateness and effectiveness of particular pedagogical strategies, and to take an active role in the evolution of subject teaching. These issues are explored further in Chapter 6.

Discursive subject mentoring takes time and it must be conducted by subject specialists who are both reflective and capable of guiding student teachers in their exploration of educational discourses. Planning discussions and lesson debriefings which access a number of educational discourses are inevitably time-consuming, and the kind of discursive subject mentoring which is advocated here for its potential to develop empowered teachers who will contribute to educational change requires an investment of time which subject mentors in the research questionnaire indicate goes way beyond the hour or so a week which they are typically allocated. Subject mentors in the study whose responses show them to be practising discursive subject mentoring are using extensive periods of time before and after school and during breaks to be able so to do. Subject mentors need further time to attend meetings and sessions with partnership subject tutors so that they can access and contribute to the exploration of subject discourses which takes place in HEI sessions.

Schools with developmental cultures in which departmental policy and practice are developed through dialogue will provide events which stimulate the kinds of thinking which discursive subject mentoring can build upon. They may also be able to provide subject mentoring departments whose members can share the role because of their joint participation in the dialogue which develops the work of individual teachers and the school. Since they value the contribution of dialogue to the development of their own practices, they are also likely to respond to the need which subject mentors have for time for dialogue. The mentoring department and the mentoring school are discussed further in Chapter 8.

6

SUBJECT MENTORING AND THE DIALOGUE OF EDUCATIONAL DISCOURSES

INTRODUCTION

This chapter argues that student teacher development incorporates dialogue with the set of educational discourses which provide the framing context for decisions made about teaching and in teaching. It is suggested that, for this dialogue to be effective, it must, first of all, be made explicit. Then, for their development to continue, student teachers must be able to engage with both the practical and theoretical formulations of these discourses. It is the task of subject mentors to facilitate, support and sometimes direct this interactive dialogue. Moreover, since this dialogue is largely conducted using verbal language, the characteristics of the language of each educational discourse must be examined by student teachers and their subject mentors.

The second part of the chapter argues that current models of teacher development pay little attention to the value of the discourses of academic subjects in the development of student teachers, particularly those following secondary PGCE courses. Most student teachers have access to these discourses at deep theoretical levels before they begin their ITE courses. Descriptions of the starting points of student teachers on these courses which ignore this expert knowledge, which often has important implications for subject pedagogy, amount to a deskilling of student teachers at the very beginning of their professional lives.

THE CHARACTER OF THE FIELD OF EDUCATIONAL DISCOURSES

Accounts of the knowledge student teachers need to access in order to teach effectively have typically described a number of 'knowledge domains' (e.g. Furlong and Maynard, 1995). This term does not do full justice to the highly significant formal debates and more informal conversations which take place in these 'domains'. These debates must be acknowledged if the most appropriate ways for student teachers to interact with them are to be determined. The term 'discourse' suggests a discussion which has a particular content and vocabulary, and a set of contributors whose power relationships have an established configuration. As Baldick (1990: 59) puts it:

> in modern cultural theory . . . the term has been used to denote any coherent body of statements that produces a self-confirming account of reality by defining an object of attention and generating concepts with which to analyse it . . . the term denotes language in actual use within its social and ideological context and in institutionalised representations of the world.

The 'object of attention' of student teachers is teaching, but they have access to numerous fairly discrete 'bodies of statements' which contribute 'concepts with which to analyse it', each of which also uses language in a way which is linked to a particular kind of 'institutionalised representation of the world'. While many of the 'bodies of statements' which are relevant to the practice of teaching overlap, it is necessary to try to identify each 'social and ideological context' which generates a 'body of statements' about teaching as a separate discourse, if subject mentors and student teachers are to be able to share a useful map of the field of discourses within which their professional thinking takes place.

Educational discourses

In Table 2, 'The theory–practice continuum in a set of related educational discourses' (see pp. 104–105), a set of educational discourses is listed. The list is inevitably incomplete, and because some of the individual discourses overlap, either in terms of their language, or their participants' power relationships, other divisions could be suggested. It is also important to acknowledge that while student teachers interact with all these discourses, they do not do so consciously at all the levels of theory and practice indicated. The educational discourses listed may be defined as follows.

The discourse of the theory of education is a conversation among philosophy, sociology, psychology and history, which compete to provide insights into the meaning and effectiveness of education.

The discourse of pedagogy explores what is meaningful and effective in education, as this can be understood from the development and analysis of educational aims, theories of teaching and learning, and the examination of individual needs in a wide range of academic and pastoral contexts.

The discourse of the academic subject explores the character, content, processes and purposes of that subject, what its meanings are, and how they are constructed.

The discourse of subject pedagogy explores how the meanings of the subject can be made accessible and taught effectively.

The discourse of the subject curriculum explores how the meanings of the subject curriculum are determined and how its effectiveness is assessed, at national, local and departmental levels, through agencies such as legislation, policy, operating procedures (including schemes of work), assessment mechanisms (including school inspections and national tests) and resources.

The discourse of the school curriculum explores how the ethos, policies, management and operational structures of the school and the subject department contribute to the meanings and effectiveness of the education of pupils in the subject.

The discourse of the classroom explores how the words and actions of the teacher and those of pupils, seen here as manifestations of their culture, knowledge, learning needs and interests, interact.

The discourse of teacher development, which explores the methods by which teachers become more effective, and the meanings generated by their teaching, is the discourse in which the ethos, practices and structures of an ITE course are defined. It is important to notice that, in the context of ITE, the discourse of teacher development is a metadiscourse since it draws attention to the concepts and practices which determine the nature of the interactions student teachers have with the other educational discourses; ITE courses also make these processes explicit to different extents.

The theory–practice continuum

The educational discourses which have been defined are individually highly complex: for example, they are conducted in terms which range from the relatively theoretical to the relatively practical; they

Table 2 The theory–practice continuum in a set of related educational discourses

Discourse	Theoretical site (example)	Theoretical (-practical) site (example)	Practical (-theoretical) site (example)	Practical site (example)
Discourse of aspects of the theory of education (e.g. history)	Critical analysis of the historical influence of the educational theories of Rousseau	Analysis of the means of applying Rousseau's theories to practice	Comparison of strategies for applying Rousseau's theories in practice	Analysis of a particular teaching situation in which Rousseau's theories were applied
Discourse of pedagogy	Comparison of Vygotskian 'scaffolding' with other theories of learning	Analysis of the effectiveness of 'scaffolding' as a means of determining practice	Critical analysis of examples of practice claiming to be based on 'scaffolding'	Devising of a teaching situation making use of the idea of 'scaffolding'
Discourse of the academic subject (e.g. English)	Comparison of reader response theory with other theories of the relationship between texts and readers	Devising a set of principles for using reader response theory in teaching situations	Comparison of the effectiveness of different lessons which were planned to make use of reader response theory	Evaluation of a lesson in which pupils were taught to apply reader response theory to a text
Discourse of subject pedagogy (e.g. English)	Critical analysis of the concept of collaborative writing in relation to cognitive theories	Critical analysis of the effectiveness of collaborative writing in terms of its impact on learning	Formulation of new teaching strategies which make use of collaborative writing	Dialogue with pupils about what they have learnt in a lesson incorporating collaborative writing

Table 2 Continued

Discourse	Theoretical site (example)	Theoretical (-practical) site (example)	Practical (-theoretical) site (example)	Practical site (example)
Discourse of the subject curriculum (e.g. English)	Analysis of ideological influences on definitions of Standard English in different NC documents	Devising a set of principles to guide practice implementing NC requirements in relation to Standard English	Comparison of the place of Standard English in schemes of work written by different school English departments	Evaluation of an attempt to assess pupils' use of Standard English in the outcomes of a scheme of work
Discourse of the school curriculum	Consideration of positive discipline in relation to findings of educational psychology	Analysis of the interpretation of positive discipline in school policy documents	Comparison of learning in lessons in which positive discipline practices were and were not used	Discussion of ways in which positive discipline practices were reinforced in a mentor's lesson
Discourse of the classroom	Analysis of the history of the development of equal opportunities awareness in education and society	Devising a set of principles for writing schemes of work which take equal opportunities issues into account	Formulation of teaching strategies for approaching equal opportunities issues with pupils of different ages	Analysis of response when a pupil prompted a classroom decision about an equal opportunities issue
Discourse of teacher development	Critical analysis of the concept of 'reflection' in comparison with that of 'competences'	Analysis of the contribution of reflection to one's own development as a teacher	Devising of questions which could be used to stimulate reflection by the teacher of a series of videotaped lessons	Use of reflection strategies in evaluating a scheme of work

have ideological, social and personal dimensions; they are locations for controversy about key matters such as the nature and development of knowledge and understanding. In Table 2, this complexity is indicated by examples of matters which access each discourse at different points on a theory–practice continuum.

The four sites indicated on the theory–practice continuum in Table 2 owe a debt to Furlong *et al.*'s (1988) description of levels of professional training, which Furlong and Maynard (1995: 52–53) acknowledge may have been more appropriately described as 'domains of professional knowledge'. The four sites also refer to the work of Zeichner and Liston (1985), which identified four types of discourse, which are very similar in character to Furlong *et al.*'s levels of training. These two sets of ideas have been used to develop definitions of some of the sites at which educational discourses may be accessed.

The term 'site' has been adopted to indicate that each access point to the field of educational discourses is of neutral status. Points of entry depend on where an academic, a teacher or student teacher is coming from, to use an appropriate metaphor, and points of departure are determined by numerous factors, including his or her intended destination, and the time, resources and people available for thinking and discussion. Some encounters with the field of educational discourses will take place at one site in one educational discourse; others will consist of journeys across many discourses and between many sites. The point is that travel is enriching; not that any particular discourse or site is somehow better than another.

At a *practical site* practical experience is questioned to reach practical conclusions, through e.g. the planning of a lesson based on the factual description of what took place in an observed or taught lesson.

At a *practical (-theoretical) site* questions which interrogate practice are used to begin to generate embryonic principles, through e.g. the comparison of different examples of practice, seeking practically applicable generalisations.

At a *theoretical (-practical) site* discussion contributes to the development of educational principles, or questions their application in practice, through e.g. the development of a set of principles which could be used to drive planning.

At a *theoretical site* principles, theories and concepts are questioned with reference to other principles, theories and concepts, through e.g. analysing whether the explanation of particular educational events in one theory is adequate.

The individual discourses in the field of educational discourses are interrelated discursively in complex ways, and this is what gives the field its conversational character. Dart and Drake (1996: 63), for example, observe that 'a student must possess certain beliefs about the subject, beliefs which are acted out in the way the student teaches, manages the classroom and establishes relationships with pupils'. Sanders (1994: 36) provides a similar example of this interrelatedness when she reports that a teacher's view of mathematics as a 'game with symbols played according to rules' not only determined how she taught mathematics but also 'the way she ran her classroom'. A student teacher's position in relation to the discourse of the academic subject taught is intimately linked to his or her position in relation to more general pedagogical discourses. Student teachers perceive that the discourses vary in the extent to which they are significant to particular teaching decisions and actions.

It is important to stress that student teachers and teachers participate in a series of written and oral interactions with other people, including government, researchers, policy makers, mentors, colleagues, parents and pupils, through which parts of educational discourses are monitored, explored and developed. Because these interactions are often literally conversations, their language is highly significant. It is also true that there are numerous other public and personal educational discourses which may influence student teachers, but which are not represented in Table 2. These include the discourses in which the media and 'outsiders' personally known to student teachers represent education.

STUDENT TEACHERS' INTERACTIONS WITH EDUCATIONAL DISCOURSES

The experiences of an initial teacher education course, however well structured to guide or sequence response and development, trigger interactions with educational discourses in ways which it is impossible to control. This is partly because of the unique background and experience of the individual student teacher, which will be discussed further later, but also because of the partial unpredictability of many aspects of school experience, particularly what happens in the classroom. Events can trigger thinking at any site on the theory–practice continuum and in any one of many relevant educational discourses. In other words, student teachers engaged in reading, discussions, simulations, planning, teaching, evaluation, reflection or decision-making may be triggered to enter one or many of the indicated educational discourses, at one or many sites on the theory–practice continuum on any particular occasion.

An example of a trigger for such interaction has been found in the documents which defined the prescribed National Curriculum for mathematics in the early 1990s. Burton (1992: 377) notes that there was a conflict in the documentation between two views of knowledge: the 'objective view of knowledge which emphasises fragmentation' and the 'constructivist' view 'termed that of the "polymath", which is more holistic, and respects individual differences'. There are, of course, accounts of teachers' knowledge which include many more categories. Sanders (1994), for example, explores the significance of 'logicist', 'formalist', 'fallibilist', 'serialist' and 'holist' as well as 'constructivist' ideas of knowledge to mathematics teaching, and Burton's argument can be seen as being limited by the binary opposition on which it is founded. However, she finds the 'constructivist' view in the statement in the *Non-Statutory Guidance to the Mathematics National Curriculum*, that 'each person's "map" of the network and of the pathways connecting different mathematical ideas is different' (NCC, cited by Burton, 1992: 378). She finds the contrasting, and perhaps contradictory, 'objective' view in many of the prescriptive requirements for skills which must be taught and tested and which are defined in the National Curriculum Statements of Attainment. Ideologically influenced contributions to the general discourse of pedagogy, which itself makes implicit reference to educational philosophy, sociology, psychology and history, impact here on the discourse of subject pedagogy in a manner which exposes the National Curriculum directive as a complex, but possibly incoherent, contribution to the subject curriculum discourse. The teacher triggered to respond to such a directive will have had to make reference to his or her own position in relation to the discourse of pedagogy, and to his or her interpretation of the discourse of his or her own classroom, in order to determine how to respond to the directive so as to create effective learning experiences for pupils.

Of course, such complex interactions are a feature of the professional lives of experienced teachers as well as student teachers. We believe that recognition of teachers' continuous interaction with a multiplicity of educational discourses confirms the complexity of teaching, and of the impossibility of reducing it to a set of competences. This complexity is extended during the act of classroom teaching, when teachers have to respond, often instantaneously, to the similarly instantaneous shifts in the relative importance of each discourse to any practical decision. In other words, teachers have to make use of what is most relevant from what they consciously or unconsciously know of these different discourses.

Wilson and Wineburg (1991) have noted the complexity, discursive inconclusiveness and variety of the knowledge held by experienced history teachers. They indicated the capacity of history teachers to hold 'different beliefs about the respective roles and responsibilities of pupils and teachers', 'different theories of learning', 'different conceptions of the history curriculum'; and to have 'different underlying conceptions of historical knowledge' and 'different configurations of pedagogical content knowledge'. From their positions in relation to this collection of educational discourses, they form a professional identity, which Shulman (1987) designates as that of the 'wise practitioner', who can draw on a collection of ideas, teaching approaches and strategies, which do not necessarily reflect a consistent educational philosophy, but rather, ongoing, deliberate participation in the discursive and fragmented conversation of educational thought. Sanders (1994: 36) provides a practical example of why this may be necessary, when she indicates that since 'successful mathematicians need to employ different views of mathematics in different situations . . . teachers of mathematics . . . have to appreciate different views of mathematics'. The flexibility of the 'wise practitioner' may be a prerequisite of effective subject teaching. However, the need for continuing interrogation of the different views of subject teaching which may be adopted at particular moments and for particular purposes must also be stressed.

LANGUAGE IN EDUCATIONAL DISCOURSES

An important aspect of the conversational character of educational discourses is the fact that they are often carried out as real conversations among members of the professional community, or between them and other groups, including parents and pupils. Many of these conversations use various forms of shorthand, such as terms which refer to: a theory of education, like 'child-centred education'; general pedagogical concepts, like 'scaffolding'; the discourse of an academic subject, like 'reader response theory'; the discourse of subject pedagogy, like 'collaborative writing'; the discourse of the school curriculum, which might refer to 'positive discipline'; the discourse of the classroom, which might include the term 'racist language'; the discourse of teacher development, like 'reflection'. In each case, these terms represent not fixed facts and concepts but highly complex educational debates: many of them are used by teachers holding different positions to mean entirely different things. Sanders (1994: 30) records the widely different interpretations of the term 'group work' she found in teachers' practice. Dart and Drake (1996: 73) significantly argue that tutors' and mentors' different philosophies often mean that definitions of competence will inevitably be interpreted differently by them, underlining the difficulty of using them in practice.

A related point is that much educational discourse, including the discourse of teacher development, is conducted in metaphorical language. The analysis of such metaphors is always informative, especially where there is a danger that they will be interpreted too literally. The best known mentoring cliché, 'Don't smile until Christmas', is, strictly, a metonym, since it identifies as representative one typical behaviour from a collection which those who advise it intend, unlike the metaphorical statement that, in traditional ITE courses, student teachers were 'thrown in at the deep end' when they went on teaching practice. However, the memorability of these statements is such that we may say with some confidence that they have influenced, respectively, the behaviour of student teachers in classrooms, and the debate about the need for new models of teacher education.

Diamond's (1991) study of the role of language in teacher development should lead us to expect this. Referring to the seminal work of Britton on language and learning, Diamond notes that 'we have to generalise from particular representations of past experiences in order to apply them to new ones' (1991: 12). As Britton put it: 'language helps us to do this by providing a ready means of classifying [our] experiences' (1975: 48). Language provides a means of making moves in the theory–practice continuum, but moves towards generalisation can screen out aspects of one speaker's practical experience in a way which may make a recipient believe that the generalisation applies to a different kind of practical experience. While generalisation is necessary to the attempt to construct principles, its limitations suggest one reason why educational discourses are never complete.

EDUCATIONAL DISCOURSES AND POSTMODERNISM

So far this chapter has stressed the complexity of the thinking undertaken by teachers and student teachers. The notion that teachers' thinking is a series of interactions with a set of educational discourses in which knowledge is always fragmented and changing, and represented in language which carries different meanings for different participants, has some distinctly 'postmodern' attributes. Wilkin (1993) has provided an analysis of 'Postmodernism as a Cultural Dynamic of Initial Teacher Training' in which she notes that certain aspects of its typical structures are indicative of a postmodern view of knowledge. Student teachers are exposed to information about, and ideas explored in, educational discourses from many sources (reading, tutors, mentors, colleagues, pupils, the media), which vary in their perspectives and levels on the theory–practice continuum (theories, concepts, 'teaching tips'), which are presented to them in many forms (lectures, discussion, simulations, observation notes, pupils' work, events in lessons), and to which they are expected to respond in many different ways (teaching, presentations, reflection, evaluation, assessment). In this continually changing context, they are expected to make decisions and act: quite simply, for example, to teach French to Year 9 at 9.20 a.m. on Monday.

Wilkin (1993: 51) argues that in a successful ITE course such postmodern attributes must interact with some 'modernist' rational certainties, such as clear definition of the roles of mentor and tutor, clear statements of goals and universal criteria against which theories can be tested. Some other commentators (see, for example, Furlong and Maynard, 1995: 50) have difficulty with the 'postmodernist relativism' of some models of ITE. However, it is quite clear that teachers are constantly required to make decisions and act in the context of partial knowledge and partial understanding. A postmodern interpretation of teaching is confirmed by the conversationally incomplete character of all educational discourses, and this is precisely what makes it impossible to maintain either that there is a reliable collection of knowledge which student teachers can simply be taught to apply, or that there can possibly be a single or simple definition of good practice for them to learn from a model. Recognition of the postmodern conversationality of educational discourses is a step towards overcoming reductive models of teacher 'training'.

111

THE POWER OF THE ACADEMIC
SUBJECT DISCOURSE

If we return to Table 2, and ask which discourse most student teachers are able to access most readily at most levels on the theory–practice continuum, the answer, for graduates embarking on PGCE courses, must be the discourse of the academic subject they have studied, and are going to learn to teach. In order to graduate, students are expected to be capable of thinking within specialist discourses at points which range from the analysis of concrete or practical examples to the abstraction of principles, and the construction, comparison or testing of theoretical positions. Furthermore, a graduate student will normally have engaged with those questions pertaining to the discourse of the academic subject which concern different ideas about its definition, content, purposes and methodology, and which stimulate consideration of the reliability and meaning of forms of knowledge generated by work within the subject. A graduate is also likely to have considered matters such as the influence of ideology on the positions taken by individual contributors to the academic subject discourse, and the relationship between that discourse and other discourses, both in related disciplines and more generally in culture and society.

Such work contributes to the generation of the high-level thinking skills which should be expected of a graduate. It is also prioritised in many fields of academic study because high status is typically accorded to 'syntactic knowledge', 'an understanding of the way a particular body of knowledge is generated and validated', in comparison to 'substantive knowledge', 'facts, concepts, key ideas' and 'an understanding of how a particular body of knowledge is structured and organised' (Furlong and Maynard, 1995: 131), not least because postmodern thinking in a wide range of academic fields questions the reliability and validity of the latter.

Just as a student teacher takes decisions and acts in either conscious or unconscious relationship to a set of educational discourses in the classroom, so an undergraduate student has operated in either conscious or unconscious relationship to an academic subject discourse, in determining the methodology of an experiment, or in choosing the analytical tools for an essay. Effective degree courses ensure that such working decisions are made explicitly and consciously, and they often do this by promoting the same kinds of reflection as ITE courses purport to stimulate.

112

A further way in which undergraduate experience indirectly prepares student teachers for the kinds of thinking which will be necessary to them in their professional role is through the close connections that exist between the syntactic knowledge of subject disciplines and subject pedagogy. Furlong and Maynard (1995: 151) acknowledge that the margins of these two kinds of knowledge are sometimes indiscernible when they indicate that 'it was not always easy to disentangle whether [student teachers'] understandings arose from an appreciation of the syntactic structures of a subject area or from their understanding of how children learn best'. In our experience, interview candidates for PGCE courses often show that they can make these connections between discourses when they are able to analyse the connections between differences in the style of subject teaching they received at A level and degree level, or perhaps from individual teachers in one of these contexts, as being linked to different conceptions of how knowledge is communicated and constructed in the subject discipline. Indeed, we expect this kind of analysis from successful candidates.

To sum up, undergraduate experience prepares students to become used to using reflection in making decisions with conscious reference to a complex discourse, to recognise the complexity of problems of knowledge and meaning, and to be capable of investigating the processes by which knowledge and meaning are constructed; the students are most confident about these skills, and most capable of using them, however, within the terms of a particular academic subject discourse.

THE SUBJECT DISCOURSE AND TEACHER DEVELOPMENT

Academic subject discourses are closely related to the subject-specific discourses of pedagogy which it is particularly important for student teachers to access. It is our contention that graduate student teachers beginning ITE courses are immediately capable of reflection and complex conceptual thinking, particularly if steps are taken to access the academic subject discourse they know best.

This view causes us to take issue with some current models of teacher development discussed earlier, at least in terms of the necessary applicability to graduate PGCE students. As indicated above, Furlong and Maynard (1995) have developed an account of student teacher development as consisting of five stages: 'early idealism', 'personal survival', 'dealing with difficulties', 'hitting a plateau' and 'moving on', each of which they perceive as having a complex set of characteristics and needs which call for mentors to prioritise certain kinds of activities. Since this work provides the most detailed account of teacher development, and because, as Furlong and Maynard indicate, it is indebted to the work of many researchers, we consider it important to devote space to an analysis of it in relation to our evaluation of the importance of subject discourses.

In Chapter 4 we discussed the first stage of student teacher development, which has been characterised as one of 'early idealism', and took issue with the notion that the first perceptions of student teachers are simplistic or naive, as described in the work of, for example, McIntyre *et al.* (1993: 97), Smith and Alred (1993: 108) and Elliott and Calderhead (1993: 169). Further, we stated our view that early idealism is linked much more positively, both to the important personal and potentially professional values student teachers bring to ITE, and to ideas which can be shown to be even more sophisticated than Furlong and Maynard suggest, if student teachers are prompted to describe them in terms of an academic subject discourse rather than discourses of pedagogy. As indicated above, successful interview candidates are often able to identify the view of the subject held by teachers they have experienced and how this view was represented in teaching actions and decisions.

For example, many English interview candidates have at some time in their education experienced a teacher who holds a 'cultural heritage' view of English (DES, 1989c), and who is mainly interested in passing on the humanistic values perceived as being located in literary texts. Interviewees can see this view as being closely linked to transmission, teacher-centred modes of teaching. They are frequently able to contrast such teachers with others who hold a 'cultural analysis' view of the subject (DES, 1989c), and who, because they are more interested in how readings of texts are constructed, actively involve pupils in constructing their own readings and exploring what considerations they have taken into account. The kind of focused idealism which emerges from this sort of sophisticated conceptual analysis can provide considerable momentum in the early part of an ITE course if it is allowed to influence actions and decisions such as the selection of teaching methods. If an English student teacher's idealism is focused on the part of the field of educational discourses indicated, it could take one of four forms: a belief in 'cultural heritage' English and the 'transmission' of knowledge; a belief in 'cultural analysis' English and the 'transmission' of knowledge; a belief in 'cultural heritage' English and 'constructivist' generation of knowledge; a belief in 'cultural analysis' and 'constructivist' generation of knowledge. After attempting to implement any of these beliefs in the classroom, the student teacher who is interacting with educational discourses at this level of consciousness can reflect on what the discourse of the classroom has had to say about the meaning of the subject and the ways in which knowledge is communicated and constructed in it. Thus, at an early stage, he or she is able to avoid a shocking clash between unfocused idealism and the realities of classroom management.

Furlong and Maynard's second stage of development is identified as 'personal survival': it is a stage in which student teachers put their idealism on hold while they overcome feelings of extreme vulnerability, by taking often largely reactive steps in order to be seen as a teacher by pupils, to fit in with the school ethos and possibly with the teaching style of their mentor, and to secure some classroom control by devising teaching strategies which reinforce discipline. While many student teachers do experience the vulnerability of this stage, student teachers who pay immediate attention to connections between their ideas about the meaning of the subject, the ways in which knowledge is constructed in it and what happens in their classrooms, are capable of making extremely rapid progress. Those student teachers who fail completely to make use of such insights tend to be the ones who become increasingly rigid, limited in the number of strategies they are prepared to try, and spend substantial parts of lessons attempting to enforce discipline. This, of course, is a vicious spiral in which pupils are demotivated by the inappropriateness of the teaching that is offered, and the absence of reference to learning made in the teachers' planning.

The mentoring approach more likely to lead to classroom success in such circumstances will not be one that concentrates the student teacher's attention entirely on rules and routines. Working on drawing out the connections between the student teacher's view of the subject and subject pedagogy by examining the learning processes he or she is attempting to promote is as important. This strategy provides an important reflective counterweight to whatever advice about classroom rules and procedures, and the provision of 'teaching tips' about strategies which are likely to work in the classroom, is necessary for the student teacher's short-term 'survival', because that kind of mentor support can very quickly undermine reflection, and create a dependency culture.

The remaining stages of Furlong and Maynard's model are linked to the constraints in the earlier stages of the models of ITE they examined. For this reason the third and fourth stages will be considered together. The third stage is called 'dealing with difficulties'. Furlong and Maynard characterise it as involving: beginning to make sense of what is happening in the classroom; trying to impress; and focusing on aspects of classroom performance, such as interactions with pupils, teaching strategies and classroom organisation. In all of these actions student teachers may be inclined to imitate their mentor. The fourth stage is called 'hitting the plateau', and is defined as a period of relative relaxation in which student teachers show some control of discipline and believe they are behaving as classroom teachers, but are not really addressing issues of teaching and learning effectively. The two stages taken together describe student teachers who adopt a limited set of strategies which they find work, which may also involve them in 'cloning' their mentor, and who rest on their laurels after having achieved this. In our view, these stages are more likely to arise when insufficient attention has been paid to the discursive complexity of teaching and learning and to the power of the subject discourse in analysis by ITE course procedures and structures.

In some ways this is confirmed by Furlong and Maynard's account of their last stage, 'moving on', in which they indicate that student teachers are challenged to re-evaluate their position and what it means for practice, that this involves asking questions about teaching and learning, and that it is met with some resistance (Furlong and Maynard, 1995: 93–95), including some which is accounted for by student teachers' reference to institutional and other constraints, and the continuing existence of other priority factors like classroom management. Although Furlong and Maynard call this stage 'moving on', their discussion usefully provides details about resistance to moving on. We would argue that this resistance is likely to be accounted for by insufficient attention to: the nature and complexity of educational discourses; the student teacher's capacity to think across the theory–practice continuum through the subject discourse; the nature of the learning opportunities which school-based initial teacher education presents in terms of allowing the student teacher to make use of ideas and information from a range of contributors to educational discourses. Re-evaluation cannot easily be superimposed on the thinking of student teachers following courses which have not made reflective evaluation a productive process from the outset.

Our experience, therefore, suggests that student teachers begin PGCE courses with sophisticated ways of seeing, and that the recognition of this can transform their development. What is needed is effective bridging of the discourse of the subject with which they are familiar to the discourse of subject pedagogy in relation to which they must act.

MENTORING AND THE DIALOGUE OF EDUCATIONAL DISCOURSES

Some of the implications for subject mentoring of stressing the significance of the student teacher's dialogue with the field of educational discourses are as follows: first, in relation to the ITE course they are involved with, mentors should always understand and, whenever possible, contribute to its presentation of the field of educational discourses to student teachers. It would be impossible to devise a one-year PGCE course which would enable student teachers to explore fully the field of educational discourses defined in Table 2. Such courses must inevitably be selective and highlight aspects of different discourses at different stages of the year, and provide entry to them at different sites on the theory–practice continuum. However, courses must also make allowances for the individual needs of student teachers, by recognising that they may be able to engage with some discourses more easily than others, and for the unpredictability of individual student teachers' experiences, by finding ways of allowing them to explore any aspect of any educational discourse when they are prompted to do so by an event.

The notion that HE tutors should remain largely responsible for theory and mentors for practice needs to be broken down. Both tutors and mentors should make explicit their understanding of the way in which the course configures its interpretation of the field of educational discourses, how the relationships between individual discourses are understood, and where they believe it is important for student teachers to focus their attention. It is particularly important for mentors to access the sophisticated thinking that student teachers are capable of in relation to their subject discourse in discussions of their most practical experience in the classroom, which mentors have much more access to than tutors.

Discussions which involve tutors, mentors and student teachers are important because they dramatise the open-endedness and searching aspects of each educational discourse by allowing different

117

voices and positions to be heard. When such discussions take place, individual topics should be located explicitly in relation to different discourses, and movement between discourses and levels of abstraction in the thinking of contributors to the discussion, at least sometimes, acknowledged.

USING THE ACADEMIC SUBJECT DISCOURSE

Because of the special knowledge that graduates have of the discourse of the academic subject they are learning to teach, it is particularly important for subject mentors to spend time exploring student teachers' academic backgrounds and interests, and discussing their learning histories in the subject, in order to establish their positions in relation to the subject discourse, and to expose connections between those positions and the student teachers' ideas about teaching and learning.

McIntyre and Hagger (1996: 158) indicate that there is research evidence that mentors and student teachers do not make good use of opportunities to explore subject discourses together, and suggest a number of reasons for this: uncertainty about roles (a partly unconscious belief that the academic subject discourse is theoretical and therefore something covered in the HEI); time (discussions of planning and lesson evaluations need to focus on the practical, which, it is assumed, does not include the academic subject discourse); power (student teachers are unwilling to question mentors' fundamental beliefs and values, and mentors feeling threatened by such questioning may feel it is inappropriate); the difficulty of separating out the academic discourse of the subject from other educational discourses. Dart and Drake (1996) similarly report a case study which showed that one student teacher's attempt to voice theoretical concerns about a lesson in terms of the academic subject discourse were rejected by a mentor, limiting the developmental scope of the debriefing.

Sanders (1994: 38) indicates that mathematics mentors may find it helpful to recall experiences in which the impact of different views of mathematics on their teaching or on dialogue about teaching was significant. These memories should be shared with student teachers. Such discussion will help mentors to identify significant references to the academic discourse of the subject in the student teacher's reflections, and to make connections to that discourse in analysis and guidance. It will also help student teachers to identify the mentor's position in relation to the academic subject discourse, which may otherwise remain hidden: failure to expose differences between the student teacher's and mentor's beliefs about the subject can potentially be a cause for failure (Dart and Drake, 1996).

We contend that the academic subject discourse has the power to be a central location for student teachers' thinking about their work; and that, while student teachers may be most confident about discussing theoretical issues in this discourse, it also has very significant practical dimensions, explaining why student teachers may begin teaching in particular ways. These points should provide sufficient grounds for the exploration of academic subject discourses to take place, even though it is time-consuming. It is the responsibility of partnership structures to ensure that the 'power' issues are overcome: student teachers should not feel that they will be judged for questioning mentors' views, and partnership events should stress the conversational quality of all educational discourses, confirming that there are no absolutely right answers.

USING THE DISCOURSE OF THE SCHOOL CURRICULUM

Mentors need to help student teachers to access the general and subject-specific educational discourses which operate in the school and in the department, and to demonstrate ways in which practising teachers make reference to both their practical and theoretical dimensions. Dart and Drake (1996) argue that this is especially important in a context of extremely rapid educational change. The quality of discussion at department meetings or internal INSET conferences is significant here, and student teachers should be encouraged to participate in the exploration of issues such as the way in which department policy responds to external theoretical and ideological influences on the curriculum.

Providing access to such discourses is a vital function of the department in mentoring. Much of the 'cloning' and many of the tendencies to narrow-mindedness recorded by Furlong and Maynard (1995) in their account of teacher development might be avoided by sufficient exposure to the range of views about subject teaching present in most departments. This also implies that departments need to learn the significance of the dialogue of discourses to teacher development. Their job is not to present a unified departmental line, unless that clearly exists, but to induct the student teacher into real educational debates. In subject areas where departments are small, and student teachers work with a limited number of practitioners, the mandatory second school experience has an important function in giving student teachers access to these debates, and mentors in both schools should work to make their differences explicit. The mentoring department has a crucial role to play in mentoring which is properly developmental.

DISCOURSE, REFLECTION AND LANGUAGE

The emphasis on conversation in the previous paragraph makes it clear why activities which give subject mentors access to the reflective processes of student teachers, and which provide records of their interactions with the discourses of education, are so important, and much more so than activities that merely check that certain competences have been achieved, or are being achieved, like monitoring lesson plans. In order to enter into the dialogue of discourses in which the student teacher participates, subject mentors need access to course journals, notes on reading which has been undertaken, and all other kinds of documentation in which reflections are recorded. Their responses to the writing of student teachers should make explicit reference to the educational discourses which the student teacher has interacted with, especially where this interaction remains implicit in the student teacher's work, or where conclusions are reached with little awareness of the arguments taking place within the relevant discourse. In relation to the points made earlier about language in educational discourses, mentors should listen out for key shorthand terminology and metaphors in the dialogue they conduct with student teachers, and look out for them in their writing. The deconstruction of such language should be encouraged so that the incomplete, conversational character of educational discourses is exposed.

CONCLUSION

This chapter has argued that attempts to understand the processes of student teacher development and to provide the means for subject mentors to support it must pay more attention to many different kinds of dialogue. First, the incompleteness of all educational discourses should be an important focus of the dialogue among HEI tutors, subject mentors and student teachers about subject teaching.

Second, the student teacher's experience, knowledge and analytical skills, particularly those which have been developed in the context of learning an academic subject discourse, should be exploited in the dialogue among tutors, subject mentors and student teachers which focuses on student teacher development. Third, the participants in these discussions should pay attention to the language in which they are conducted, and make explicit the interactions of different discourses in their thinking and their classroom practice.

7

DISCURSIVE SUBJECT
MENTORING AND
COLLABORATIVE TEACHING

INTRODUCTION

This chapter explores a key practice now central to, and common among, many HEI courses: collaborative teaching. Some of the opportunities which collaborative teaching presents for ITE are discussed. The discussion makes reference to the study of subject mentors introduced in Chapter 5, and to a case study of a collaborative teaching activity. The case study of a collaboratively taught English lesson is analysed, identifying the educational discourses described in Chapter 6, which discursive subject mentoring can access.

Subject mentors in the study indicated that they regard their approaches to collaborative teaching as making an effective contribution to the development of student teachers. They recognised the importance of shared planning and debriefing in making collaborative teaching effectively developmental for student teachers, and while they were very positive about the benefits of these processes, they indicated that the time available for them was not always sufficient to take full advantage of their possibilities. However, their responses showed that they believed that collaborative teaching is most effective in terms of its benefits to school pupils: this aspect of its operation was perceived as much less problematic.

Most subject mentors also reported that they saw collaborative teaching mainly as a step towards whole class teaching, which could be abandoned once a certain level of classroom competence has been achieved. This view was confirmed by subject mentors' tendency to revert to using it more often when student teachers develop difficulties in the classroom. This practice is surprising, both because the value of collaborative teaching to pupils was considered to be very high, and because many subject mentors also felt that it led to more productive debriefing sessions and better professional relationships with student teachers than formal classroom observation. In fact, subject mentors' perception that the time available for planning collaborative teaching declines when student teachers have a larger 'solo' teaching commitment often seemed to be the most significant factor in its decreasing use as time goes on.

A small minority of subject mentors were opposed to collaborative teaching on principle. Their argument was that it creates 'unrealistic' classroom situations, which shield student teachers from the more demanding problems which they have to learn to handle independently. They also felt that collaborative teaching encourages them to learn teaching strategies which have no possible application without two adults in the classroom. The position argued in this chapter builds from the overwhelming evidence in most subject mentors' experience that shared planning and debriefing of collaborative teaching are even more effectively developmental than lesson observation debriefing is. It will be suggested that the special opportunities of collaborative teaching force student teachers to challenge views of the teacher as a monolithic transmitter of information, and have a beneficial influence on their conception of the relationships between teachers, pupils and knowledge. Collaborative teaching is of such value to all participants in ITE partnerships, including pupils, that it should be pursued throughout school placement time. The chapter begins with a discussion of subject mentors' uses of and opinions about the effectiveness of the following aspects of collaborative teaching: collaborative teaching modes, shared planning, the benefits to pupils and debriefing.

COLLABORATIVE TEACHING MODES

In general, subject mentors indicated that they make use of a wide range of collaborative teaching strategies. These strategies can be broadly categorised as follows.

Teacher and classroom assistant mode

In this mode, either the subject mentor leads teaching and the student teacher assists, or vice versa. The classroom assistant role is often either to support individual pupils, with the less able often singled out for particular attention, or to ensure that there is 'better coverage' of small groups while they are working on a task.

Subject mentors indicated that this mode provides good opportunities for them to 'model' teaching when they lead a lesson, or to use some formal observation techniques when the student teacher is leading. In both cases, the 'assistant' can gain better insight into aspects of pupil learning, such as their understanding of and engagement with tasks, by becoming directly involved in the classroom. Having a clear lead teacher also helps pupils who are not used to collaborative teaching to understand where authority lies in the lesson.

Linear sequence mode

In this mode, the lesson is compartmentalised into sections for which the subject mentor and student teacher take separate responsibility, agreed in advance.

Subject mentors indicated that this mode enables student teachers to focus on particular aspects of whole class teaching, either by carrying them out or by observing the subject mentor's strategies. This mode is used most frequently when student teachers take their first steps in whole classroom teaching, to draw attention to the issues involved in matters such as: settling a class, introducing a topic, effecting a transition, conducting a demonstration, working an example, or using questions. In this mode, it may be harder for pupils to identify the 'lead teacher', and its rigid structure may inhibit spontaneity (if, for example, the subject mentor curtails an activity which is found to need more time so that the 'student teacher's time' for another activity is not diminished).

Pre-teaching observation mode

In this mode, the student teacher watches the subject mentor teach and then uses the same material with another class.

Subject mentors indicated that this mode can usefully draw attention to the need to modify teaching strategies with different groups of pupils, and to the flexibility which is needed to respond to the unpredictability of classroom events. However, the teaching skills demonstrated by the subject mentor need to be internalised and made transferable by the student teacher, which takes time. The danger is that, without this internalisation process, this practice can lead to bland copying and 'cloning', unsatisfactory lessons and student teacher demoralisation. Shared planning (see below) is an important step towards avoiding this pitfall.

Planning/teaching split mode

In this mode the student teacher plans a lesson which the subject mentor then teaches or vice versa.

Subject mentors indicated that this mode makes interesting use of the dynamics created by the student teacher's ideas and the subject mentor's experience, and that the process is particularly useful for developing strong professional trust. Although the independent planning which takes place in this mode might appear to overcome some of the time problems associated with effective collaborative teaching, the 'planner' still needs to brief the 'teacher' sufficiently well for the lesson to be taught with a sense of ownership, and debriefing is as important as in any other mode.

Class division mode

In this mode, the class is divided into two groups which are then taught separately by the subject mentor and student teacher for periods ranging from parts of a lesson to the duration of a scheme of work.

Subject mentors found that this mode had benefits for pupils in terms of increased individual attention, and that it is an effective means of freeing the student teacher from some of the classroom management concerns of whole class teaching. Subject mentors who had used this mode to give student teachers access to work with examination classes tended to be most enthusiastic about it. Shared planning and debriefing continue to be crucial if the experience is to be developmental.

All of these collaborative teaching modes can also be undertaken by pairs of student teachers working together, or by student teachers working with their HEI tutors, although the nature of the learning experience and the impact on pupils is modified by these working arrangements. This chapter will confine itself to student teacher/ subject mentor collaborations.

PROBLEMS WITH COLLABORATIVE TEACHING MODES

Apart from planning time problems, the most frequently reported difficulty subject mentors had in making collaborative teaching effective concerned authority in the classroom. For some, this centred on the student teacher's relationship with the subject mentor: 'There is always the problem of shared leadership, with a student teacher usually relinquishing charge to the member of staff for fear of "treading on toes" by asserting herself.' For others, the problem centred on pupils' perceptions of what is happening: a number of subject mentors indicated that younger pupils in particular needed the source of authority to be more clearly defined than collaborative teaching allowed. However, some comments suggested that other subject mentors had overcome this problem by making the collaborative teaching process explicit to pupils: 'You need to make it obvious which teacher is leader and which is subordinate at each stage of the lesson.' This comment clearly refers to positive experience of the linear sequence mode of collaborative teaching, in which the problem is likely to be most serious.

Some subject mentors indicated that collaborative teaching only works when the relationship between subject mentor and student teacher really 'gels', and the discussion of debriefing below certainly confirms the importance of a strong professional relationship. However, this professional closeness is not as necessary for some of the modes of collaborative teaching described above as others. Some subject mentors and student teachers are able to operate very flexibly, with both parties happy about the other intervening spontaneously, whereas other pairings can only make the linear sequence mode work because responsibilities are very clearly demarcated in it. Explicit discussion of the available options can sometimes help partners establish working practices which suit them. Awareness is an issue here, because although, as indicated above, subject mentors collectively use a wide range of strategies, many individual subject mentors who responded to the research questionnaire reported using only one.

PLANNING

In all of the collaborative teaching modes described above, except the planning/teaching split mode, either the subject mentor or student teacher can plan the lesson and brief the other, or shared planning strategies can be used. Subject mentors expressed a strong view that shared planning makes collaborative teaching most effective, but that time constraints put limits on how often this practice can be used. As one subject mentor put it: 'It is necessary to set aside a substantial period of time for this; to outline a scheme of work, discuss, go away and consider, meet again and pool ideas, discuss practical details, etc. This is essential if the student teacher is to feel "ownership" of the topics/approaches used and therefore, have full commitment to them.'

Despite this time difficulty, subject mentors described two main groups of benefits from shared planning, which are clearly of potential value to student teachers and subject mentors throughout a PGCE course, rather than only when student teachers are beginning to be active in the classroom.

The first group of benefits concerns *the refinement of student teachers' planning*. Subject mentors argue that the active sharing of planning allows them to focus student teachers' thinking more effectively on particular aspects of it. The timing of parts of lessons, which is of particular importance in the linear sequence mode of collaborative teaching, and often an early problem for student teachers, was the focus most frequently mentioned by subject mentors. Differentiation, which the teacher and classroom assistant mode provides special opportunities to address, and which student teachers tend to become more effective in planning for later in their development, was also mentioned by a number of subject mentors.

The second group of benefits concerns the building of what one subject mentor called a 'two-way learning process' for student teachers and subject mentors. At their best, 'joint planning sessions are joint learning sessions' to which the student teacher contributes fresh approaches and new ideas, and the subject mentor contributes the expertise of years of practical experience. Several subject mentors indicated that such exchanges are important in building effective professional relationships.

BENEFITS TO PUPILS

Subject mentors were so positive about the benefits to pupils of collaborative teaching that they ranked them sixth in effectiveness out of thirty-two aspects of partnership in the research questionnaire, and backed this assessment up with enthusiastic comments: 'one of the most valuable aspects of partnership from the school's point of view'.

Subject mentors listed and described a large number of different perceived benefits, which can, however, be placed in two distinct groups. Most subject mentors described the benefits as being related to various aspects of *pupil support*, or what one subject mentor called the 'better coverage' which is achieved in the teacher and classroom assistant mode of collaborative teaching. Student teachers were seen as particularly useful in this support role in many different kinds of classrooms and activities by different subject mentors: A level, GCSE, Key Stage 3, mixed-ability work, group work, projects, practicals, open-ended investigations, individual tasks, oral assessment and IT were all mentioned by at least one subject mentor, suggesting that this usefulness is really universal. A few subject mentors indicated that placing student teachers in this role had enabled them to make use of the expertise which they bring to the course: 'The strengths and specialisms of students have particularly helped exam pupils.' Acknowledging such expertise affirms the graduate status of student teachers, which is especially important at the start of their school experience.

However, it is in relation to the second set of perceived benefits, which can be grouped together as *extending perspectives on learning*, that student teachers are able to transform classroom learning much more radically. Examples of this benefit described by subject mentors include 'providing two views of material' and 'introducing discussion into the presentation of material'. Such strategies add variety and novelty to lessons, 'it is much more interesting to have two voices', but they also enable teachers to make particularly effective moves away from transmission modes of teaching, in which knowledge may be perceived by pupils as 'given', towards ones in which knowledge can more readily be seen to be constructed, and in which classroom discourse is turned into real dialogue. English, Science and History subject mentors reported using collaborative teaching to set up debates, sometimes in which one adult could be primed to 'demonstrate an effective or ineffective argument', but more frequently to suggest different possible interpretations of evidence. History subject mentors (most frequently) had used student teachers to take on characters with different viewpoints in role play. Modern Languages subject mentors indicated the value of 'pupils hearing the target language used for real communication'.

DEBRIEFING COLLABORATIVE TEACHING

A high proportion of subject mentors in the survey indicated that lesson debriefing is more effective after collaborative teaching. Many subject mentors commented that the 'mutual trust' which arises from shared responsibility for a lesson 'allows for openness of comment'. The procedure is seen as both stimulating honesty and dependent on it: 'The student teacher and subject mentor have to be able to see areas which could have gone better, regardless of who was responsible.' In addition to this strengthening of the professional relationship, a number of subject mentors indicated that the shared experience of teaching allowed more probing analysis to take place. Both participants 'know' the lesson in a manner which is unique to the teacher of a solo lesson, something which can lead to reticence in criticisms of observed lessons, however constructively they are voiced.

Some subject mentors saw this shared knowledge as making the communication of *their* perspective on the work easier to communicate; one wrote: 'I can explain where I make mistakes or use strategies it might be difficult for a less experienced teacher to employ.' However, a larger number stressed the 'more equal relationship' and 'two-way discussion about learning outcomes'. Subject mentors mentioned both the value of debriefings which consisted of real dialogue, 'similarities and differences in the *experience* of the lesson form the basis for discussion', and that access to this experience meant that it was easier to talk about 'why things were done as they were'. Both participants were seen as gaining deeper insight: 'being involved helps the subject mentor to understand specific problems' and so give the student teacher more effective guidance. One subject mentor said this dialogue, while less objective than an examination of the evidence of competence recorded by a formal lesson observation, enabled participants to achieve 'more realism about problems in real teaching'. Another said it 'helps to review the lesson collectively, not just the specific role of the teacher'. An integrated discussion of the dynamics of teaching and learning processes is more valuable than a mechanistic assessment of competences, which focuses too much on what the teacher does.

These observations challenge the claim that subject mentors should operate primarily as experienced guides and advisers, like the Ancient Greek character Mentor, which is sometimes made in defining what a subject mentor ought to be (e.g. Stephens, 1996: 1). The subject mentors in the study stressed that the student teachers' perspective in the dialogue in which they participate with subject mentors is as valuable as their own. One subject mentor acknowledged that such dialogue teaches subject mentors as much as student teachers by enabling them to 'actually see what has gone on – you can use it to assess your own effectiveness'. Collaborative teaching at its best sets up forms of dialogue which are suited to a postmodern context

129

in which all participants can learn from offering and receiving fragmentary knowledge and impressions which are acknowledged to be incomplete.

The evidence from the research questionnaire is that collaborative teaching works best when it has a genuinely conversational character. This is true both of its operation in the classroom, where it can be used to set up forms of dialogue which challenge the concept of teacher as transmitter of information, and of the subject mentor/student teacher conversations which are generated by it. In other words, the evidence suggests that collaborative teaching is effective precisely because, when it is led by mentors who have the time and skills to work discursively, it stimulates the kinds of dialogue which it has been argued in Chapter 6 are particularly valuable in ITE.

CASE STUDY

In the case study which follows, the capacity of collaborative teaching to extend perspectives on learning was exploited in a particularly sophisticated use of the linear sequence mode. However, the analysis offered is intended to focus attention on the field of educational discourses which dialogue between subject mentors and student teachers can access in order to promote student teacher development.

Description

As part of a scheme of work in which William Armstrong's (1973) novel *Sounder* was used as a class reader, a student teacher in the first term of his PGCE secondary English course explored the possibilities of collaborative teaching in preparing pupils to write a newspaper article. In the novel, a 'negro' who is accused of stealing meat is sent to a boot camp. The idea of the lesson was to create a press conference at which pupils taking the role of journalists are informed of the theft and the prejudiced suspicions of the Deputy Sheriff and the owner of the smoke house from which the meat was stolen.

The format of the activity was adapted from a model lesson which had been delivered in a college Subject Studies session, the student teacher having noticed its potential for collaborative teaching. The student teacher's notes indicate that the teaching sequence ran as follows:

1 **Introduction:** Teachers will give two statements in role – one from the Deputy Sheriff and one from the owner of the smoke house. Pupils will act as reporters and will be able to ask questions. Working in groups of four, pupils will work on producing a draft of a newspaper article about the theft.   **5 mins**

2 Statements from student teacher in role and subject mentor in role.   **5 mins**

3 Questions from 'reporters' to student teacher and subject mentor.   **5 mins**

4 Group work on newspaper article.   **25 mins**

5 Teacher issues Fax from FBI with new information on the case.   **10 mins before end**

Evaluation

An analysis of the student teacher's reflective evaluation of this lesson shows how his thinking made contact with a number of educational discourses. It also shows that the imaginative use of the subject mentor in role made in this collaborative lesson was linked with the student teacher's views of learning and of his subject in a way which bridges these discourses.

The *discourse of pedagogy* is engaged with when the student teacher makes reference to ways in which the strategies of the lesson stimulated pupil response and involvement. For example, the student teacher notes: 'After reading the statement, questions were invited from the floor, which the pupils seized on with a "need to know" attitude. This engagement helped the pupils formulate their ideas very effectively.' A 'constructivist' view of learning and knowledge is implied here.

The *discourse of the academic subject* is engaged with in the student teacher's references to the concept of representation, which is important in media education. He comments that the point of the presentation of two views of the same events by himself and his subject mentor in role was that 'Different people respond in different ways and it was essential that this was expressed to the pupils.' In fact, the pupils were called upon to recognise both that witnesses to an event will always read it differently from their unique perspectives, and that journalists impose a further perspective through their selection and interpretation of the witnesses' evidence.

The student teacher's assignment includes the plans for the next lesson, which supported pupils in the development of an understanding of their task as 'journalists', before they completed their writing task, by examining the complex ways in which meaning is constructed in newspapers. In this lesson pupils looked at the representation of a single event in a number of different articles. The student teacher comments: 'It was important at that stage in their learning that I took a step back in terms of their understanding of the nature of newspaper journalism.' At the centre of the learning experience which is provided here is a view of English as concerned with the processes by which interpretations of events and texts are constructed, and this underlies the student teacher's view that the lesson on newspapers was necessary.

The *discourse of subject pedagogy* is engaged with when the student teacher makes connections between his sense of the ways in which interpretations are constructed and the method used to teach the pupils. Comparing the collaborative teaching strategy he and his subject mentor used with the 'model lesson' taught in college, the student teacher comments: 'I felt that the lesson would really benefit from two different voices.'

Another part of the discourse of subject pedagogy could be accessed through discussion of the student teacher's decision to hold the lesson on newspaper articles *after* the role play lesson, although the sequence is not something his evaluation comments on explicitly. Accounts of the teaching of writing place different degrees of emphasis on the importance of paying attention to *writing processes* such as notemaking and drafting, which the first lesson stresses, and teaching about *genres*, here newspaper articles, which the second lesson stresses (see, for example, the discussion in Parker, 1993). The sequence chosen by the student teacher is intended to ensure that the pupils have collected and can manipulate content before they are shown how to mould this to the constraints and possibilities of a particular genre. Redrafting is given the clear role of developing form.

The *discourse of the subject curriculum* is engaged with when the student teacher makes a precise reference to the requirements of the National Curriculum which were best met by the work in the lesson. He quotes: '"Pupils should be encouraged to listen attentively both in situations where they remain silent, and where they have the opportunity to respond immediately"' (DfE, 1995: 17). In fact, the work in the lesson breaks down this rather rigidly expressed distinction and creates a more dynamic learning experience: the silent listening is used to collect the information which makes considered responses possible.

The *discourse of the classroom* is addressed when the student teacher describes how discipline was reinforced during the initial statement he gave in role as Deputy Sheriff. The student teacher wrote himself a script for this which began:

> Good morning. I'd like to welcome y'all to this hastily arranged press conference. I trust y'all are aware of why we are gathered here so I'll get straight on with the facts as they are now. My name is Jefferson P. Mulrone Jnr and I am the Deputy Sheriff of Wichita State County's Law Enforcement. I will answer any of your questions at the end of this press conference but I do not like to be interrupted so shut up until I have finished speaking. Is that clear?

The student teacher indicates that, because of this statement, 'the pupils knew what their listening expectations were'. This interesting comment demonstrates the student teacher's confidence that pupils will recognise and respond to the language of classroom discipline when it is disguised as subject content. Many drama teaching books state the importance of teachers who work in role beginning with roles which carry an authority equivalent to their own (for example, O'Neill *et al.*, 1977). This guidance suggests the capacity of pupils to understand, and on occasion find enjoyment in, the cross-referencing of different educational discourses in the classroom.

The *discourse of the school curriculum* is engaged with when the student teacher observes ways in which the lesson extended itself beyond his objectives: 'the strategies I used provided a stimulating discussion, subtly, about racism, which was a bonus because it was something I hadn't anticipated . . . one or two of the pupils really berated me for my "attitude".' This comment suggests that the pupils' engagement with the work enabled them to make an important leap across the gap between different educational discourses: they were not just 'learning how to write a newspaper article' or 'learning about the class reader'. Their learning was more vibrant and substantial because it concerned the exploration of important human values which inform the whole school curriculum.

The *discourse of teacher development* is engaged with in a number of ways. First, the student teacher demonstrates that this discourse is not just one he experiences, but one which he is capable of stepping outside and analysing: he headed his assignment 'A Reflection on a Model of Collaborative Teaching' and he shows that he has constructed his model from the 'example of a teacher in role lesson' he had experienced in a Subject Studies session and his own ideas about the opportunities of collaboration: 'I took it a stage further and used myself in role . . . and also the class's normal teacher in role.' His capacity for effecting a synthesis of this kind is impressive, and it is also a demonstration of the kind of creative thinking which is often necessary in classrooms.

In the student teacher's lesson evaluation these references to different educational discourses are not made explicit or isolated from each other. They form part of a rich, fluid analysis of the student teacher's intentions and their relationship with the outcomes he believed were achieved. Perhaps one reason why the student teacher was able to marshal references to so many different discourses into a single piece of reflection was because of the clarity of his 'constructivist' thinking. This thinking connects his general assessment of the way in which the opportunity to construct knowledge stimulates pupils, and his implied beliefs that English is about the construction of meanings and interpretations, and that classroom methodology should contribute to the communication of this central tenet of his practice.

SUBJECT MENTOR INTERVENTION IN THE DIALOGUE OF DISCOURSES

The evaluation provided a rich frame of reference for potential developmental intervention by the subject mentor, which could have focused the student teacher's attention on aspects of any of the discourses he mentioned.

Thus, the observations centred in the *discourse of pedagogy* could be used to begin an examination of ways in which the teacher's role can be modified to allow knowledge to be constructed by pupils, in lessons which are still based on whole class teaching strategies. Those centred in the *discourse of subject pedagogy* could be used to stimulate an exploration of other ways in which multiple viewpoints can be represented in the classroom, or different approaches to the sequencing of writing activities which pay attention to genre and drafting processes. Those centred in the *discourse of the academic subject* could be used to stimulate discussion about the openness of texts to the construction of different interpretations (e.g., How far does the text of *Sounder* seek to bring about anti-racist responses in its readers, and is this a matter to explore with pupils?). Those centred in the *discourse of the subject curriculum* could be used as a stimulus for an exploration of the relationship between individual National Curriculum requirements and the integrated classroom practice the student teacher adopted. Those centred in the *discourse of the classroom* could be used to promote discussion of other ways of establishing discipline indirectly, or pupils' ability to read across different educational discourses. Those centred in the *discourse of the school curriculum* could concern a discussion of the need for alertness to lesson content which will provoke pupils to think and speak about sensitive issues, and ideas about explicit and implicit anti-racist teaching. All of the issues identified here have been used to enter the field of educational discourses at what we have called practical(-theoretical) sites (see above, Chapter 6), and could be explored with more theoretical or more practical emphasis, depending on the student teacher's ability to conceptualise or to translate theoretical ideas into practice when thinking in any particular discourse, on his practical needs, and on the time and resources available.

The subject mentor's task in responding to a verbal or written evaluation of the kind analysed in this case study is to help student teachers to make explicit the references to different discourses in their thinking, and to help them to prioritise ideas and issues to pursue. The analysis above suggests the complexity of this task, which is further complicated by the need to take into account the student teacher's stage of development and the development needs which PGCE course structures make a priority.

This chapter has suggested that time for debriefing is of fundamental importance here and that a subject mentor's active involvement in the process of a collaboratively taught lesson improves the effectiveness of such debriefing time. It is important, also, not to forget that student teachers will often show considerable initiative in identifying the issues which it is most important for them to pursue. The student teacher whose work this case study has explored, for example, followed this assignment up with an investigation of the provision for using texts from other cultures in the English department and the school library. He selected and isolated the aspects of the work which were to do with the discourse of the school curriculum, and pursued those systematically.

135

CONCLUSION

Unquestionably, the majority of subject mentors in the study saw the benefits of collaborative teaching for pupils despite the fact that the time available for them was not always sufficient to take full advantage of their possibilities. Those mentors who were able to engage in a range of collaborative activities found that they developed not only the student teacher's practice, but also their own. Furthermore, we would argue that collaborative teaching is of such value to all participants in ITE partnerships, including pupils, that it should be pursued throughout school placement time. Subject mentors can contribute to the effectiveness of collaborative teaching in school-based ITE by taking steps to ensure that, in the context of the partnerships to which they belong:

- the model of student teacher development adopted makes available a variety of modes of collaborative teaching, the characteristics of which should be made explicit and used as a basis for selection in particular circumstances;
- opportunities are taken to use collaborative teaching to extend perspectives on learning as well as to place student teachers or subject mentors in pupil support roles;
- the benefits to pupils, and those of the two-way dialogue between student teachers and subject mentors, are understood as having value throughout the periods of student teachers' school placements;
- it is understood that the effectiveness of collaborative teaching is dependent on the availability of substantial periods of time for planning and evaluation, and that these are made available to subject mentors;
- the debriefing of collaborative teaching, and other lessons, identifies individual educational discourses as a means of giving evaluation structure and promoting the targeted further development of student teachers.

8

THE MENTORING SCHOOL
AND THE MENTORING
DEPARTMENT

INTRODUCTION

Subject mentoring in schools is still in its infancy and understandings of the processes of mentoring are still growing and will continue to grow in coming years. The discussion of mentoring in this book has been presented in the hope that it will further the understanding of the processes of subject mentoring for mentor and tutor alike, and suggest further areas for research. This book has argued that learning to become a teacher is not just about the acquisition of competences. Professional competence rather involves a capacity to theorise from practical experience, and to interpret theory in practical situations. Moreover, teachers think across the theory–practice continuum in dialogue with a complex, interrelated set of educational discourses. The development of the capacity to do this is vital because it enables teachers to become creative, flexible and hence properly resourceful, and it provides a basis for professional development that can extend beyond ITE experience.

In school-based ITE, subject mentors can play a key role in developing teachers who have this capacity, particularly if they adopt the practices of discursive mentoring. However, discursive mentoring cannot easily be introduced and sustained by individual mentors on their own. In this chapter, the role of the mentoring school in supporting subject mentoring will be considered with reference to the concept of the Professional Development School that has recently been influential in the USA. The characteristics of the mentoring subject department will then be discussed.

THE MENTORING SCHOOL

Discursive mentoring is a time-consuming activity. The results of the study described in Chapter 5 show that subject mentors regard lack of time as the most significant constraint on their effectiveness. These results confirm the findings of, among others, Glover and Gough (1995), Kelly *et al.* (1992) and Mardle (1995). Subject mentors who adopt discursive mentoring practices are frequently using large amounts of their own time to do so. Schools whose practices already encourage the kind of high-quality professional dialogue which explores a range of educational discourses, and whose staff are prepared to give student teachers access to this dialogue, are likely to be able to support discursive mentoring particularly well. Such schools will immerse student teachers in a culture that is professionally sympathetic to it. Such schools are also likely to be more responsive to the need to provide subject mentors with an appropriate allocation of time for their task.

This connection between effective subject mentoring and whole school culture has been made by some researchers and practitioners in the USA, who have promoted the concept of the Professional Development School (PDS). In the last fifteen years, this idea has been generated in the context of the moves towards school–HE partnership models of ITE in the USA. There has been steady progress in this direction, although the speed of change has varied from state to state and programme to programme. Some of the key stages in the process of change have been as follows. The involvement of 'master [*sic*] teachers' in the design and delivery of ITE programmes was an influential recommendation of *A Nation at Risk* (1983), a report published by the National Commission on Excellence in Education which stimulated moves towards a major restructuring of the US education system. The importance of developing ITE courses which integrate school and HE experience and create effective links between theory and practice as part of this restructuring was recognised in publications such as the Holmes Group's report *Tomorrow's Teachers* (1986).

The influential Holmes Group defines itself as 'A Consortium of Research Universities Dedicated to Improving Teacher Education and the Profession of Teaching': it has published two further reports, *Tomorrow's Schools* (1990) and *Tomorrow's Schools of Education* (1995), each of which has argued a stronger case for more integrated school–HE partnership. Although debate continues about what form partnership should take, and some writers have been critical of the Holmes Group's position (Labaree, 1995; Gideonse, 1996), there is a consensus view in the USA that ITE needs to respond to the research indications that student teachers were finding the greatest value in the school-based components of their courses, and that they were often unable to make effective connections between the theory taught in HE institutions and the practical teaching problems they faced in the classroom (Slick, 1995a). Integrated teacher preparation has consequently become a cornerstone of educational reform.

It is now widely recognised in the USA that the role of school-teachers, traditionally and still most often called 'cooperating teachers', is highly significant in determining the effectiveness of school-based experience in ITE (Brennan, 1995). A 1994 national survey of school principals (Slick, 1995b: 103–125) found that 29 per cent of schoolteachers supporting student teachers are now called mentors, and that teachers who are effective mentors are regarded as the second most important critical aspect in the operation of school experience, or 'field experience' programmes. (The preparation of student teachers for the experiences was the aspect perceived to be more important.)

The importance of student teachers having extended purposeful, structured experiences in schools, beginning early in their courses, is also now widely recognised (Bercik, 1991; Wilson, 1996). This need is being met through the development of a wide range of activities, usually termed 'field experiences', which have been defined as including: 'classroom observations, tutoring, assisting school administrators or teachers, participation in school and community-wide activities, student teaching and internships' by the National Council for the Accreditation of Teacher Education (1992, cited by Slick, 1995a: xxiv). NCATE is an agency whose accreditation standards for the institutions it inspects respect the consensus view that 'field experiences are a necessary and valuable part of preservice education' (Ribich, 1995: 36).

Depending on their interpretation of reflective practice, US researchers suggest a range of strategies for the promotion of dialogue and reflection in the school experience component of ITE. These include the keeping of personal logs and diaries, autobiographical writing, the use of metaphor and imagery, group discussion, ethnographic study, the consideration of models of teaching, techniques of prompting in supervision practices, action research, and curriculum analysis and development projects (Copeland et al., 1993).

Some recent research emphasises ways in which mentors should structure different kinds of school experience to promote reflection. For example, Werner *et al.* (1995) suggest the need to provide trigger questions to help student teachers structure the thinking in reflective logs, and indicate that the logs can then become a resource for individual dialogue with tutors, bridging the gap between the private and social aspects of reflection. Some other strategies suggested draw attention to the need for evidence to be assessed as objectively as possible in reflection. For example, a mentor may provide a formal spoken or written commentary on a video of student teacher practice in the classroom (Werner *et al.*, 1995). Strategies for the structured analysis of audiotapes of lessons and for involving pupil assessment of lessons put greater responsibility on the student teacher (Freiberg, 1995), but still need monitoring by the mentor. Emphasising the social dimension of reflection further, Glatthorn and Coble recommend 'reflective practice seminars' (1995: 31) which involve student teachers, mentors and tutors in discussion of current curriculum issues, and activities such as the analysis of videos of student teachers' practice.

To sum up, the importance of the role of the mentor in school-based ITE is as strongly recognised in the USA as it is in Britain. American research recommends a range of mentoring practices, many of which promote dialogue in which student teachers are expected to take an active role, and through which they are expected to engage with a number of educational discourses. A number of these practices make heavy demands of mentors, especially in terms of time. It has been recognised that subject mentors and student teachers benefit from the support of a school culture which is sympathetic to their need to have extended opportunities for discussion.

PROFESSIONAL DEVELOPMENT

The concept of the Professional Development School (PDS) has been developed in an attempt to define the most appropriate locations for 'field experience'. The term was introduced in *Tomorrow's Schools* (1990) to describe a site for total collaboration between school and HE teachers. The report's idealistic definition indicates that a PDS should be: first, a laboratory of practice, in which good practice is demonstrated and problems are researched; second, a site of continuous professional and curriculum development; and third, a location for preparing preservice teachers (Holmes Group, 1990; Labaree, 1995). The Holmes Group has been criticised for undermining other kinds of educational research and for proposing to create schools with artificial conditions (Labaree, 1995). Moreover, the concept of the PDS has been interpreted in many different ways, and the quality of its contributions to ITE has been equally variable (Goodlad, 1993; Zeichner, 1990). However, the debate has led to useful attempts to define authentic collaboration, and to create visions of what could result from it. Goodlad (1993, Figure 1) calls for:

1 the creation of exemplary school sites;
2 the creation of internships and residencies through which future educators may observe and gain experience with the best possible educational practices;
3 the development of curricula that reflect the best analyses and projection of what young people need;
4 the assurance of equal access by all students to these curricula;
5 the cultivation of site-based development activities designed to foster continual school renewal;
6 the continuous infusion of knowledge relative to good education in schools and in programs preparing educators.

US experience suggests that numerous benefits would accrue to school and HE teachers, as well as student teachers, if a large number of schools could become PDSs in full realisation of Goodlad's vision. Indeed, his own research indicates that the willingness of a school to enquire critically into, and seek renewal of, its own current practices is crucial to the effectiveness of field experience (Goodlad *et al.*, 1990 cited in Slick, 1995a). Goodlad's concept of the PDS incorporates elements which would allow for an apprenticeship model of ITE, such as the demonstration of 'best possible educational practices', but he emphasises the ideas that practice can always be further developed, and that the 'infusion of knowledge' contributes to such practical development work. He recognises the importance of the incompleteness of educational discourses and their straddling of the theory–practice continuum. The PDS is defined in a way which suggests that it should be a location in which the developmental dialogue of discursive mentoring can flourish.

While Goodlad's criteria should not be used to establish a limited number of élite ITE schools, they do offer a vision of the kind of school culture which is needed in the current British context, in which the role of schools in promoting Continuing Professional Development, as well as in providing substantial support for ITE, is likely to be extended. The vision of teachers, student teachers and

141

HE tutors approaching school and curriculum development together, all contributing particular kinds of experience and expertise in a problem-solving framework, is a powerful one. It would be appropriate for schools involved in ITE partnerships to evaluate their performance in relation to Goodlad's criteria, and to target some aspects of those criteria in their development plans, as one means by which quality in partnerships could be generally improved.

There is a growing body of evidence in the United Kingdom of the benefits to schools from an involvement with ITE. Such involvement, it is argued, creates a development culture which promotes consistent practice across departments and allows for effective communication across the school (Holmes, 1992). Elsewhere, Evans (1995) maintains that mentoring can be a 'significant stimulus' for the mentor's own professional development. Further, based on school development projects, some have argued for the creation of a system of peer mentoring and support as an effective model of on-going staff development (Featherstone and Smith, 1992). Such a system, it is believed, might underpin all aspects of a school's work, particularly in the light of curricula or policy innovation, which is planned, implemented and evaluated collaboratively and openly in a climate of mutual trust. If the processes of such collaboration are beneficial to the development of a student teacher or NQT, then there are clear benefits for the experienced teacher from peer mentoring and being mentored by a peer. Such a system of staff development provides a teacher with a colleague who can discuss, share and question practice in order that both parties develop professionally in what Kelly *et al.* (1992) refer to as the 'learning school'.

The promotion of the benefits to school development by an involvement in ITE has also been made in the Teacher Training Agency's series of four working papers, *Effective Training Through Partnership* (TTA, 1996c). One of the 'key principles' of Working Paper 3, 'Maximising the Benefits of Partnerships', states that a school involved in ITE is more likely to be a 'learning school' and thus more able to improve its performance. Indeed, the paper notes that 'considerable benefits for individual teachers, for a group of teachers or department, for the school as a whole and for clusters of schools are becoming increasingly evident' (p. 8). Working Paper 3 goes on to assert that one of the actual and potential benefits of whole school involvement in ITE is the establishment of a development culture which focuses on 'improving teaching and thus improving pupils' learning' (p. 10).

THE MENTORING DEPARTMENT

The TTA's fourth working paper states clearly that the school subject department is the most important context in which student teachers can experience a development culture. Such a culture reflects Goodlad's aims for the Professional Development School. However, the responses to the research questionnaire described in Chapter 5 indicate that some subject mentors interpret the idea of incorporating student teachers into the subject department much more in terms of functions which they are expected to take on. This attitude was represented in comments such as: 'we involved her in the Christmas play'; 'he helped to organise a school concert'; and 'she was a valuable source of help on a recent theatre trip'. Involvement in such activities undoubtedly introduces student teachers to an important aspect of a teacher's work, and prepares the ground for key aspects of professional development. However, this work needs to be carried out alongside full participation in professional dialogue which engages with a range of educational discourses. Dart and Drake (1996: 68) found that little dialogue between subject mentors and student teachers addressed the cross-section of views which exist about the teaching of any subject. They make the important point that lack of dialogue between subject mentors and student teachers can have a bearing on assessment: 'Implicit beliefs may be influencing the overall judgment about the student's competence.'

More positively, our research indicated that many subject mentors do recognise the importance of introducing student teachers to a departmental culture in which teachers are permanently engaged in curriculum development discussions that draw on a wide range of theoretical and practical considerations. The quotations below are from subject mentors who place a high value on discussion, who believe that departments and student teachers can constructively share each other's professional problems and development needs, and who consequently operate what may be called 'discursive mentoring departments': 'Students are very much encouraged to regard themselves as members of staff and are invited to become as involved as possible'; 'initially, the whole department guided the student teacher with her project ideas'; 'expectations of various sorts are discussed at department and other meetings attended by student teachers'; 'within the department we share ideas and knowledge on all aspects of the subject'; 'discussion is the key – highlighted by all of the department'; 'student teachers are given department documents as a basis for discussion'; 'student teachers have been involved in many initiatives and have attended many meetings which have broadened their understanding'. One subject mentor summed up her approach to mentoring and the way in which she believed she might best help student teachers to develop: 'through enthusiasm for subject, suggested materials, methods. This is undertaken by the whole department, who love nothing better than to talk about any aspect of the subject.'

Where discussion really is the key to departmental practice and development, subject mentors see the value of incorporating student teachers fully in departmental/faculty meetings, departmental INSET, examination board and moderation meetings, and parents' evenings. Each of these kinds of meeting gives student teachers access to a situation in which a different educational discourse may be prioritised. Department meetings may be more concerned with the place of subject teaching in the discourse of the school curriculum, whereas departmental INSET may be more concerned with exploring subject pedagogy: attending both kinds of meeting will enable student teachers to see the constraints and possibilities which apply to the subject curriculum in a particular school. Attendance at examination board and moderation meetings will give student teachers access to the discourse of the subject curriculum, and at the same time as they are learning about matters such as National Curriculum or GCSE requirements and standards, they will discover ways in which these standards are problematic. For instance, when there is a disagreement about the grade which an examination board has awarded a piece of exemplar work, student teachers may be alerted to differences of opinion about what qualities should be most rewarded in assessing the subject they are learning to teach. They will see that these different views are sometimes related to profound beliefs about what the subject is and means. Attendance at parents' evenings gives student teachers insights into the relationships between what teachers believe to be good practice in subject teaching and the expectations of parents, which may be based on their understanding of the presentation of the curriculum and other educational issues in the media. These activities taken together provide an insight into the ways in which teachers constantly move among the educational discourses which are relevant to the teaching of their subject, depending on the context, and demonstrate their capacity to engage with these discourses at levels which are determined by matters such as the time available, their audience, and their aims in a particular discussion.

Through access to discussions of this kind, student teachers will also come to understand that, in any department, there can be a wide range of views about the importance of different aspects of the subject, a diversity of opinions about subject pedagogy, and a variety of teaching styles, all of which are informed by the values and beliefs of individual members. Shared aims and goals may allow a range of these views to be expressed to pupils over time, or may be represented by core schemes of work which individual teachers then interpret, at least to some extent, differently. Once student teachers are aware of the existence of such discussions, they can begin to see their own classrooms as locations in which they are engaged in the same kinds of educational exploration as their more experienced colleagues. They may also understand something of how and why shared departmental policies have been determined, which will enable them to implement those policies critically. Perhaps most importantly, they may learn that one of their future roles will be to contribute to the formulation of departmental policy, some showing that they are able to do this while still at their placement schools.

CONCLUSION

In Part II of the book we have emphasised the importance of subject mentoring as opposed to the importance of the subject mentor. This distinction has been deliberate. While we wish to acknowledge that there are personal skills, qualities and attributes which might be identified as comprising or exemplifying a *good* mentor and that positive professional relationships between student teacher and subject mentor are of significance, it is the processes of mentoring which, we argue, are of most importance. From what has gone before, it is clear that we believe there are real benefits for student teachers, mentors and pupils to gain from the processes of discursive mentoring. Unquestionably, discursive mentoring takes time and it must be conducted by subject specialists who are both reflective and capable of guiding student teachers in their exploration of educational discourses. The time problem is extremely significant and many subject mentors in our study felt that the lack of protected allocated time for mentoring activities was a major constraint. However, it is clear that schools with developmental cultures in which departmental policy and practice are developed through dialogue will provide events which stimulate the kinds of thinking which discursive mentoring can build upon. They may also be able to provide departments whose members can share the mentoring role because of their joint participation in the dialogue which develops the work of individual teachers and the school.

At the same time we acknowledge that the development of whole department approaches to mentoring is not unproblematic, as, for a variety of reasons, not all colleagues would wish to be involved in ITE. There is a need for departmental clarity about the expectations and roles of its members in relation to such an enterprise. (For a discussion of the constraints and possibilities of departmental involvement in mentoring see, for example, Dart and Drake (1996); Evans (1995); Glover and Gough (1995); Mardle (1995).) Nevertheless, while we do not wish to suggest that all teachers are, or should be, mentors, there is evidence from our study that whole department involvement in mentoring (and in particular, in discursive mentoring) is beneficial not only for the student teacher, but for the subject department, the school and its pupils. As one subject mentor said, summing up the benefits for all involved in discursive mentoring: 'Connecting ideas makes things livelier, richer.'

Part I of this book was critical of the philosophy underpinning the establishment of the Teacher Training Agency and of some of its early pronouncements, which appeared to indicate a determination to remove HEIs from any involvement in Initial Teacher Education. However, the publication of the Agency's working papers *Effective Training Through Partnership* (TTA, 1996c), perhaps signals a shift in attitude. The series of four working papers was produced by a task group on which schools, HEIs, LEAs and HMI were represented. Such a group provides a forum of the kind which appeared to be lacking in the early 1990s when ITE policy was being reworked. As a consequence of the composition of the group, the working papers acknowledge, through their definitions of 'key principles' and 'issues to consider', the complexities involved in teacher development. Moreover, the model of teacher development which underpins the papers' exploration and exemplification of good practice in school–HEI partnerships is firmly anchored in reflective practice. Working Paper 3 (TTA, 1996c: 8–11) clearly articulates the benefits to all teachers of 'having to reflect' on practice. Further, the paper argues the benefits of 'closer and more productive relationships between schools, HEIs and LEAs' and of 'regular [teacher] contact with staff from the HEI, which improves teachers' access to, and understanding of, current best practice and research'.

In their paper on mentoring practice, Featherstone and Smith (1992: 153) state the importance of the ethos of a school in creating a development culture. It 'depends on the right atmosphere, that is, a climate where there is mutual trust, respect and confidence'. The TTA is the government agency most charged with the oversight of ITE. The production of its *Effective Training Through Partnership*, through discussion involving all interested parties, may well indicate a shift from dictate to dialogue with teacher educators in schools and HEIs, which can only take place in the type of climate described by Featherstone and Smith. Whether this change will also characterise the development of future education policy by government remains to be seen. Clearly, the TTA and teacher educators believe there are benefits to be gained by the teaching profession as a whole from the post-1992 arrangements for secondary teacher education. This book has argued that such benefits are the result of a model of teacher education which recognises the complexities involved in learning to teach; which acknowledges that teaching is not a value-free activity and that mentoring involves teachers in the socialisation of student teachers into a profession, rather than training entrants only in the development of skills. If, as a result of a particular ideological position, there is a further attempt to reduce teacher education only to training in the acquisition of a simple set of 'context-free' skills, then we put at risk not only the quality of teachers produced by such 'training', but also the quality of the education that pupils will receive. Skilled technicians 'delivering' the National Curriculum will not develop the critical thinking needed by pupils to face the demands of life in the next century.

It is vital that ITE partnerships work to develop approaches to teacher education which acknowledge the complexity, discursive inconclusiveness and variety of the knowledge held by teachers. Partnerships should resist the notion that there is either a reliable collection of knowledge which student teachers can simply be taught to apply, or a single or simple definition of good practice which they can learn from a model. The development in both pre-service and in-service teachers of the habit of critical reflection on their own teaching and learning is much more likely to result in the development of similar critical thinking in their pupils. We advocate the promotion of the discursive subject mentoring department as the key location for this kind of teacher development.

APPENDIX A

Areas of competence expected of newly qualified teachers in Northern Ireland

Extract from: Department of Education Northern Ireland (1996) *Arrangements for Initial Teacher Education in Northern Ireland from September 1st 1996.*

The competences have been assigned letter codes to indicate the stages at which most attention will be given to their development:

'A' indicates initial training;
'B' induction; and
'C' the early years of further professional development.

A capital letter is used to signify the stage of training during which the competence will mainly be developed; a lower case letter indicates that the stage will play a subsidiary (though still significant) role in developing the competence in question.

A 5-point scale is used to indicate the relative weight placed on school-based work (SBW). The indications are as follows:

1 little or no school-based work is needed;
2 though some school-based work will be needed, much of the development can take place outside the school;
3 the competence can be developed by a roughly equal balance of school-based work with other guidance;
4 the main emphasis should be on school-based work, but with some other guidance also;
5 the whole development of the competence can be achieved within the school.

Competences   SBW   Stage

1 Understanding of the Curriculum, and Professional Knowledge

Demonstrates knowledge of child development, spiritual, moral, intellectual, physical, social and emotional, and understanding of how it can be promoted.	2	A
Demonstrates knowledge of the various ways in which children learn, both generally and in particular subject contexts.	2	A
Demonstrates understanding of social, psychological, developmental and cultural influences on children's attainment.	2	A
Demonstrates knowledge of the role of language in learning.	2	Ab
Demonstrates understanding of the learning which can take place through non-verbal means.	2	Ab
Demonstrates understanding of the range and importance of play for learning.	2	Ab
Demonstrates understanding of the importance of motivation, attitude to schooling and the dynamics of peer group influence in the promotion of effective learning.	3	aBc
Demonstrates knowledge of the principles involved in fostering good discipline.	3	aBc
Demonstrates understanding of the importance of assessment as an integral part of teaching and learning.	2	aBc
Demonstrates awareness that there are differing views about the aims of education.	1	A
Demonstrates awareness of contemporary debates about education.	2	Ac
Demonstrates knowledge of the part of the education system in which he or she is working and its relationship to other parts of that system.	1	Ab
Demonstrates understanding of the relationship between the education system and other aspects of society.	1	A
Demonstrates general knowledge of the history and context of education in the UK and particularly in Northern Ireland since 1947.	1	A
Demonstrates understanding of the appropriate provisions of the Education Reform (Northern Ireland) Order 1989 and of other relevant legislation.	1	Ab
Demonstrates knowledge of the organisation and management	3	aBc

149

of schools, and the place within these of school policies and development plans.

Contributes to the formulation of the school's aims and objectives.	5	bC
Demonstrates understanding of schools as institutions and their place within the community.	1	Ac
Demonstrates understanding of the arguments in favour of a balanced and broadly-based curriculum.	1	A
Demonstrates awareness of the extent to which learning in schools takes place outside the formal curriculum ('the hidden curriculum').	2	Ab
Demonstrates knowledge and understanding of the requirements of the Northern Ireland Curriculum, and in particular of the areas of study and the educational themes embodied in it and of their interdependence.	2	Abc
Demonstrates knowledge of the range of resources available to support the curriculum.	2	aBc
Demonstrates understanding of the ways in which information technology contributes to children's learning.	3	Abc
Demonstrates awareness of the skills and processes common to a range of subjects.	3	abC

2 Subject Knowledge and Subject Application

Demonstrates understanding in depth, of the knowledge, concepts and skills of his or her specialist subject(s), going beyond the immediate demands of the school curriculum for the relevant age-phase.	1	A
Demonstrates breadth of knowledge in all of the subjects forming the content of his or her teaching.	1	Ab
Demonstrates knowledge of the relationships between different subjects and their contribution to areas of study.	1	A
Plans appropriate lessons within teaching programmes.	3	Ab
Demonstrates a knowledge of the particular methodologies and procedures necessary for effective teaching of the subject(s) forming the content of his or her teaching.	3	Ab
Shows awareness of potential areas of learning difficulty within the subject(s).	4	Ab
Plans and employs a variety of teaching strategies to the subject or topic.	3	Abc

Uses an appropriate combination of thematic and subject approaches.　　4　aB

Prepares coherent teaching programmes, taking into account statutory requirements for both the subject(s) and the educational themes, and school curriculum policies.　　4　abC

Can justify the selection of material in terms of curricular principles and child development.　　2　aC

Understands how to organise field work and exploit its educational potential.　　3　abC

3 Teaching Strategies and Techniques, and Classroom Management

Plans and employs a wide range of teaching strategies appropriate to the age, ability, interests, experiences and attainment level of the pupils and to the objectives of each lesson.　　4　aBc

Can justify the teaching methods being used.　　3　Ab

Demonstrates awareness of individual differences among children – the uniqueness of each child – the needs which arise from these.　　3　aBc

Takes account of pupils' diversity of talents.　　4　aBc

Is able to recognise pupils' special needs and provides appropriately for these.　　4　aBc

Takes account of cultural differences among children.　　4　aBc

Contributes to ensuring continuity and progression in children's learning within and between classes and subjects.　　5　abC

Teaches in whole class, group, pair or individual modes as appropriate for particular learning experiences.　　3　Abc

Manages play and activity-based learning when appropriate.　　4　Ab

Is able to make a smooth transition between different learning activities or lessons.　　4　Ab

Encourages pupils to develop powers of observation and inquiry.　　4　aBc

Creates appropriate problem-solving situations in which pupils can exercise newly acquired skills.　　3　aBc

Is able to prepare appropriate learning materials for pupils.　　3　Ab

Captures and maintains pupils' attention, interest and involvement.　　4　aBc

Maintains pupils' motivation.　　4　Ab

Contributes to the development of pupils' language and communications skills, reading, numeracy, information handling and other skills.   3   abC

Makes pupils aware of appropriately demanding expectations for their progress.   4   abC

Encourages pupils to take initiatives and become responsible for their own learning.   4   abC

Questions pupils effectively, responds and supports discussion.   3   Ab

Makes appropriate use of the range of available resources.   4   Ab

Uses information technology to enhance children's learning.   3   aBc

Deploys a range of strategies to create and maintain a purposeful, orderly, safe and appropriate environment for . learning   4   aBc

Establishes good classroom rapport by providing a pleasant, psychologically secure and stimulating environment in which each pupil may progress, grow in confidence and develop a positive self-image.   4   aBc

Establishes clear rules and expectations for pupil behaviour.   4   aB

Pre-empts inappropriate pupil behaviour and confrontation.   5   aB

Deals with inappropriate pupil behaviour, within the policy of the school, by an appropriate use of investigation, counselling, academic help, rewards and punishments.   5   aB

Manages his or her own time and that of the pupils effectively.   4   aBc

Manages space effectively through awareness of a variety of classroom layouts.   4   aBc

Is able to make effective use of non-teaching staff.   5   aB

Seeks advice when necessary.   5   B

Demonstrates awareness of the importance of informed critical reflection in evaluating his or her professional practice.   2   Abc

Demonstrates understanding of the effects on children's learning of teachers' expectations, including those which may arise from stereotyping.   2   Ab

4 Assessment and Recording of Pupils' Progress

Demonstrates understanding of the nature and purposes of the different kinds of assessment which may be used.   2   Ab

Assesses and records pupils' performance in a systematic manner, using attainment targets and level descriptions where applicable.   3   aBc

Judges pupil performance against appropriate norms, taking due account of the character of the intake of the school. 3 abC

Uses different methods of assessment as appropriate in order to monitor the progress of individual children. 3 aB

Participates in moderation procedures within the school. 5 Bc

Demonstrates an awareness of children's extra-curricular achievements. 5 B

Uses the outcomes of assessment, as appropriate, in order to evaluate teaching and plan for the future. 4 C

Provides pupils with regular thorough feedback on their progress in a constructive manner which fosters their self-confidence and self-esteem. 4 Ab

Encourages pupils to play a positive part in their own assessment. 4 aB

Provides helpful reports to parents on their children's progress. 4 Bc

5 Foundation for Further Professional Development

Accepts and undertakes the pastoral responsibilities of a teacher. 5 aBc

Liaises, when appropriate, with members of other professions concerned with the welfare of pupils. 5 abC

Demonstrates knowledge of his or her contractual, legal, pastoral and administrative responsibilities. 2 aBc

Demonstrates awareness of how to respond to current social problems which may manifest themselves in schools. 2 aC

Demonstrates understanding of how to draw upon sources of professional help and expertise. 3 aB

Demonstrates awareness of his or her role as a member of a professional team within the school. 5 abC

Relates effectively with parents. 4 Bc

Develops effective working relationships with teachers and other colleagues within the school and, where applicable, in associated schools. 5 bC

Contributes to cross-curricular aspects of school work. 3 aBc

Contributes to activities with pupils outside the formal curriculum. 5 abC

Takes appropriate responsibility for curriculum leadership. 3 bC

Communicates effectively, where appropriate, with representatives of the community of which the school is a part. 5 C

APPENDIX B

Core criteria underpinning judgements about student teacher progress in each of the five areas of professional competence

Extract from: Department of Education Northern Ireland (1996) *Arrangements for Initial Teacher Education in Northern Ireland from September 1st 1996.*

These are the underlying qualities of the teacher which enable him or her to pull together the individual competences and apply them in the professional context.

A Professional Values

A person who:

- likes and cares for children, and seeks to promote the development of the whole child;
- is enthusiastic about teaching and is committed to the value of the educational process;
- believes in the promotion of equal opportunities, recognising differences occasioned by race, religion, sex, class or disability, but adopting non-discriminatory policies in all these respects;
- accepts the role of parents in the educational process;
- possesses high professional standards.

B Professional Development

A person who:

- engages in self-appraisal and critical evaluation of his or her work;
- engages in professional development both as an individual and through working constructively and in a spirit of collegiality with others in the professional context;

154

- keeps up to date with relevant aspects of his or her subject(s);
- is open to the possibilities of change and innovation.

C   Personal Development

A person who:

- has a lively mind and a range of cultural, intellectual and other interests;
- has self-confidence arising from the ability to give a reasoned justification for actions;
- shows a willingness to learn;
- shows perceptiveness and insight.

D   Communications and Relationships

A person who is:

- able to communicate easily and effectively;
- able to establish and maintain constructive relationships with children, colleagues, parents and others;
- sensitive to the emotional dimension of interaction with children and others.

E   Synthesis and Application

A person who is able to:

- implement, plan, manage, organise and evaluate to ensure learning;
- integrate a wide range of knowledge and skills;
- apply knowledge and skills appropriately and effectively in practical situations.

REFERENCES

Alexander, R. (1984) *Change in Teacher Education* London: Holt, Rinehart & Winston.

Armstrong, W. (1973) *Sounder* London: Puffin.

Ashworth, P.D. and Saxton, J. (1990) 'On Competence', *Journal of Further and Higher Education*, 14 (2), 15–27.

Avis, J. (1994) 'Teacher Professionalism: One More Time', *Educational Review*, 46 (1), 63–72.

Baldick, C. (1990) *The Concise Oxford Dictionary of Literary Terms* Oxford: Oxford University Press.

Barber, M. (1996) *The Learning Game: Arguments for an Education Revolution* London: Gollancz.

Beardon, T., Booth, M., Reiss, M. and Hargreaves, D. (1992) *School Led Training* Cambridge: Cambridge Occasional Paper, Cambridge University Education Department.

Benton, P. (ed.) (1990) *The Oxford Internship Scheme: Integration and Partnership in Initial Teacher Education* London: Calouste Gulbenkian Foundation.

Bercik, J.T. (1991) 'Teacher Education and Development of a Proactive/ Reflective Pre Service Program', *Education*, 112 (Winter), 200–205.

Berliner, D. (1994) 'Teacher Expertise', in Moon, B. and Shelton Mayes, A. (eds) *Teaching and Learning in the Secondary School* London: Routledge.

Bhatia, V. K. (1993) *Analysing Genre: Language Use in Professional Settings* London: Longman.

Bolton, E. (1994) 'The Quality and Training of Teachers', in *Insights into Education and Training* Paul Hamlyn Foundation, National Commission on Education, London: Heinemann.

Bonnett, M. (1996) 'New Era Values and the Teacher–Pupil Relationship as a Form of the Poetic', *British Journal of Educational Studies*, 44 (1), 27–41.

Brennan, S. (1995) 'Making a Difference for Student Teachers through the Careful Preparation of Supervisors', in Slick, G. (ed.) *Making the Difference for Teachers* Thousand Oaks: Corwin.

Bridges, D. and Kerry, T. (eds) (1993) *Developing Teachers Professionally: Reflections for Initial and In-service Trainers* London: Routledge.

Britton, J. (1975) 'Language and Learning', in Bullock, A. *The Bullock Report: A Language for Life* London: HMSO.

Brown, S. (1996) 'School-Based Initial Teacher Education in Scotland: Archaic Highlands or High Moral Ground?', in McBride, R. (ed.) *Teaching Education Policy: Some Issues Arising from Research and Practice* London: Falmer Press.

Burton, L. (1992) 'Becoming a Teacher of Mathematics', *Cambridge Journal of Education*, 22 (3), 377–386.

Busher, H. and Saran, R. (eds) (1995) *Managing Teachers as Professionals in Schools* London: Kogan Page.

Calderhead, J. (1987) 'The Quality of Reflection in Student Teachers', *European Journal of Teacher Education*, 10 (3), 269–278.

Calderhead, J (1989) 'Reflective Teaching and Teacher Education', *Teaching and Teacher Education*, 5 (1), 43–51.

Calderhead, J. (1992) 'Induction: A Research Perspective on the Professional Growth of the Newly Qualified Teacher', in *The Induction of Newly Appointed Teachers* General Teaching Council for England and Wales, Berkshire: NFER.

Calderhead, J. and Gates, P. (eds.) (1993) *Conceptualising Reflection in Teacher Development* London: Falmer Press.

Calderhead, J. and Robson, M. (1991) 'Images of Teaching: Student Teachers' Early Conceptions of Classroom Practice', *Teaching and Teacher Education*, 7 (1), 1–8.

Carr, D. (1993a) 'Guidelines for Teacher Training: The Competency Model', *Scottish Educational Review*, 25 (1), 17–25.

Carr, D. (1993b) 'Moral Values and the Teacher: Beyond the Pastoral and the Permissive', *Journal of Philosophy of Education*, 27 (2), 193–207.

Carr, D. (1993c) 'Questions of Competence', *British Journal of Educational Studies*, 41 (3), 253–271.

Carr, W. and Kemmis, S. (1986) *Becoming Critical: Education, Knowledge and Action Research* London: Falmer Press.

Chappell, C. and Hager, P. (1994) 'Values and Competency Standards', *Journal of Further and Higher Education*, 18 (3), 12–23.

Cooper, P. and McIntyre, D. (1996) *Effective Teaching and Learning* Buckingham: Open University Press.

Copeland, W.D., Birmingham, C., De La Cruz, E. and Lewin, B. (1993) 'The Reflective Practitioner in Teaching: Toward a Research Agenda', *Teaching and Teacher Education*, 9 (4), 347–359.

Council for the Accreditation of Teacher Education (CATE) (1992) *The Accreditation of Initial Teacher Training under Circulars 9/92* (DfE) and 35/92 (Welsh Office) London: CATE.

Dart, L. and Drake, P. (1996) 'Subject Perspectives on Mentoring', in McIntyre, D. and Hagger, H. (eds) *Mentors in Schools: Developing the Profession of Teaching* London: Fulton.

Day, C. (1995) 'Leadership and Professional Development: Developing Reflective Practice', in Busher, H. and Saran, R. (eds) *Managing Teachers as Professionals in Schools* London: Kogan Page.

Department of Education and Science (DES) (1984) *Initial Teacher Training: Approval of Courses Circular Number 3/84* London: DES.

DES (1985) *Better Schools* London: DES.
DES (1988) *Qualified Teacher Status: A Consultation Document* London: DES.
DES (1989a) *Articled Teacher Pilot Scheme: Invitation to Bid for Funding* London: DES.
DES (1989b) *Initial Teacher Training: Approval of Courses* London: DES.
DES (1989c) *National Curriculum: English for Ages 5–16* London: HMSO.
DES (1992a) *Speech by Secretary of State to North of England Conference* London: DES.
DES (1992b) *Reform of Initial Teacher Training: A Consultation Document* (CATE criteria) London: DES.
Department for Education (DfE) (1992) *Initial Teacher Training (Secondary Phase) Circular Number 9/92* London: DfE.
DfE (1993a) *The Government's Proposals for the Reform of Initial Teacher Training* London: DfE.
DfE (1993b) *The Initial Training of Primary School Teachers: New Criteria for Courses*, Circular Number 14/93 London: DfE.
DfE (1995) *English in the National Curriculum* London: HMSO.
Department for Education and Employment (DfEE) (1996) Press Release 12 June 1996, 192/96 London: DfEE.
Department of Education Northern Ireland (DENI)(1991) *Teachers for the 21st Century: A Review of Initial Teacher Training*, Consultation Paper Bangor: DENI.
DENI (1993a) *Review of Initial Teacher Training (ITT) in Northern Ireland: Reports of Three Working Groups* Bangor: DENI.
DENI (1993b) *Review of Initial Teacher Training (ITT) in Northern Ireland: Reports of the Development Group* Bangor: DENI.
DENI (1996) *Learning for Life: Arrangements for ITT in Northern Ireland from 1 September 1996* Bangor: DENI.
Dewey, J. (1933) *How We Think: A Restatement of Reflective Thinking in the Educative Process* Boston: Heath.
Diamond, C. (1991) *Teacher Education as Transformation* Philadelphia: Open University Press.
Downie, R. S. (1990) 'Profession and Professionalism', *Journal of Philosophy of Education*, 25 (2), 147–159.
Eisner, E. (1982) *Cognition and Curriculum* London: Longman.
Elbaz, F. (1992) 'Hope, Attentiveness and Caring for Differences: The Moral Voice of Teaching and Teacher Education', *Teaching and Teacher Education*, 8 (5/6), 421–432.
Elliott, B. and Calderhead, J. (1993) 'Mentoring for Teacher Development: Possibilities and Caveats', in McIntyre, D., Hagger, H. and Wilkin, M. (eds) *Mentoring: Perspectives on School-Based Teacher Education* London: Kogan Page.
Elliott, J. (1989) 'Teacher Evaluation and Teaching as a Moral Science', in Holly, M.L. and McLoughlin, C.S. (eds) *Perspectives on Teacher Professional Development* London: Falmer Press.
Elliott, J. (ed.) (1993) *Reconstructing Teacher Education: Teacher Development* London: Falmer Press.

REFERENCES

Eraut, M. (1994) *Developing Knowledge and Competences* London: Falmer Press.

Evans, T. (1995) 'The Departmental Perspective', in Glover, D. and Mardle, G. (eds) *The Management of Mentoring* London: Kogan Page.

Everard, B. (1995) 'Values as Central to Competent Professional Practice', in Busher, H. and Saran, R. (eds) *Managing Teachers as Professionals in Schools* London: Kogan Page.

Everton, T. and White, S. (1992) 'Partnership in Training: The University of Leicester New Model School-Based Teacher Education', *Cambridge Journal of Education*, 22 (2), 143–155.

Fairclough, N. (1992) *Critical Language Awareness* London: Longman.

Fairclough, N. (1995) *Media Discourse* London: Edward Arnold.

Featherstone, B. and Smith, S. (1992) 'Peer Support as the Basis of Good Mentoring Practice', in Wilkin, M. (ed.) *Mentoring in Schools* London: Kogan Page.

Field, B. (1994) 'The New Role of the Teacher-Mentor', in Field, B. and Field, T. (eds) *Teachers as Mentors: A Practical Guide* London: Falmer Press.

Field, B. and Field, T. (eds) (1994) *Teachers as Mentors: A Practical Guide* London: Falmer Press.

Freiberg, H. (1995) 'Promoting Reflective Practices', in Slick, G. (ed.) *Emerging Trends in Teacher Preparation* Thousand Oaks: Corwin.

Frost, D. (1993) 'Reflective Mentoring and the New Partnership', in McIntyre, D., Hagger, H. and Wilkin, M. (eds) *Mentoring: Perspectives on School-Based Teacher Education* London: Kogan Page.

Fuller, F. and Bown, O. (1975) 'Becoming a Teacher', in Ryan, K. (ed.) *Teacher Education, 74th Year Book of the National Society for the Study of Education* Chicago: University of Chicago Press.

Furlong, J. (1995) 'The Limits of Competence: A Cautionary Note on Circular 9/92', in Kerry, T. and Shelton Mayes, A. (eds) *Issues in Mentoring* London: Routledge.

Furlong, J. and Maynard, T. (1995) *Mentoring Student Teachers* London: Routledge.

Furlong, V., Hirst, P., Pocklington, K. and Miles, S. (1988) *Initial Teacher Training and the Role of the School* Milton Keynes: Open University Press.

Gideonse, H. (1996) 'Holmes Group III: Responsible in Goals, Remiss in Practicalities', *Journal of Teacher Education*, 47 (Mar/Apr), 147–152.

Glatthorn, A. and Coble, C. (1995) 'Leadership for Effective Student Teaching', in Slick, G. (ed.) *The Field Experience* Thousand Oaks: Corwin.

Glover, D. and Gough, G. (1995) 'Interaction and Impact', in Glover, D. and Mardle, G. (eds) *The Management of Mentoring* London: Kogan Page.

Glover, D. and Mardle, G. (eds) (1995) *The Management of Mentoring* London: Kogan Page.

Goodlad, J. (1990) *Teachers for Our Nation's Schools* San Francisco: Jossey-Bass.

Goodlad, J. (1993) 'School–University Partnerships and Partner Schools', *Educational Policy*, 7 (Mar), 24–40.

Goodlad, J., Soder, R. and Sirotnik, K. (eds) (1990) *Places Where Teachers Are Taught* San Francisco: Jossey-Bass.

Graham, J. and Barnett, R. (1996) 'Models of Quality in Teacher Education', *Oxford Review of Education*, 22 (2), 161–178.

Griffiths, M. and Tann, S. (1992) 'Using Reflective Practice to Link Personal and Public Theories', *Journal of Education for Teaching*, 18 (1), 69–84.

Habermas, J. (1974) *Theory and Practice* London: Heinemann.

Hagger, H., Burn, K. and McIntyre, D. (1993) *The School Mentor Handbook* London: Kogan Page.

Hargreaves, D. (1989) 'PGCE Assessment Fails the Test', *Times Educational Supplement*, 3 November.

Hartley, D. (1993) 'Confusion in Teacher Education: A Postmodern Condition?', in Gilroy, P. and Smith, M. (eds) 'International Analyses of Teacher Education', *Journal of Education for Teaching*, 19 (4), 89–93.

Her Majesty's Inspectorate (HMI) (1987) *The New Teacher in School* London: HMSO.

HMI (1991) *School-Based Initial Teacher Training in England and Wales* London: HMSO.

Hillgate Group (1989) *Learning to Teach* London: Claridge Press.

Hillman, J. (1994) 'Undergraduate Perceptions of Teaching as a Career', in *Insights into Education and Training* Paul Hamlyn Foundation, National Commission on Education, London: Heinemann.

Holmes, S. (1992) 'Assessment and the Licensed Teacher', in Wilkin, M. (ed.) *Mentoring in Schools* London: Kogan Page.

Holmes Group (1986) *A Report of the Holmes Group: Tomorrow's Teachers* Michigan: The Holmes Group.

Holmes Group (1990) *A Report of the Holmes Group: Tomorrow's Schools* Michigan: The Holmes Group.

Holmes Group (1995) *A Report of the Holmes Group: Tomorrow's Schools of Education* Michigan: The Holmes Group.

Hopkins, D. (1996) 'Penetrating the Dark Matter in Secondary Schools', Keynote address to Exploring Futures in Initial Teacher Education Conference, University of London Institute of Education, 21 September.

Hoyle, E. (1995) 'Changing Conceptions of a Profession', in Busher, H. and Saran, R. (eds) *Managing Teachers as Professionals in Schools* London: Kogan Page.

Hoyle, E. and John, P.D. (1995) *Professional Knowledge and Professional Practice* London: Cassell.

Husbands, C. (1993) 'Profiling of Student Teachers: Context, Ownership and the Beginnings of Professional Learning', in Bridges, D. and Kerry, T. (eds) *Developing Teachers Professionally: Reflections for Initial and In-service Trainers* London: Routledge.

Husbands, C. (1994) 'Integrating Theory and Practice in Teacher Education: The UEA Model of Action-Research Based Teacher Education', in Field, B. and Field, T. (eds) *Teachers as Mentors: A Practical Guide* London: Falmer Press.

Hutchinson, D. (1994) 'Competence-Based Profiles for Initial Teacher Training and Induction: The Place of Reflection', *British Journal of Inservice Education*, 20 (3), 303–312.

Hyland, T. (1993) 'Professional Development and Competence-Based Education', *Educational Studies*, 19 (1), 123–132.

Hyland, T. (1996) 'Professional, Ethics and Work-Based Learning', *British Journal of Educational Studies*, 44 (2), 168–180.

Jaworski, B. and Watson, A. (eds) (1994) *Mentoring in Mathematics Teaching* London: Falmer Press.

Jessup, Q. (1991) *Outcomes: NVQs and the Emerging Model of Education and Training* London: Falmer Press.

Jones, L. and Moore, R. (1993) 'Education, Competence and the Control of Expertise', *British Journal of Sociology of Education*, 14 (4), 385–398.

Kellett, C. (1994) 'Towards More School-Based Initial Teacher Education', in Field, B. and Field, T. (eds) *Teachers as Mentors: A Practical Guide* London: Falmer Press.

Kelly, A.V. (1995) *Education and Democracy: Principles and Practices* London: Paul Chapman.

Kelly, M., Beck, T. and ap Thomas, J. (1992) 'Mentoring as a Staff Development Activity', in Wilkin, M. (ed.) *Mentoring in Schools* London: Kogan Page.

Kerry, T. and Shelton Mayes, A. (eds) (1995) *Issues in Mentoring* London: Routledge.

Kleinberg, S. (1993) *Key Ideas and Issues Concerning Mentoring and How They Affect One B.Ed. Course,* Report Commissioned by SOED, Glasgow: Strathclyde University.

Knaub, R. (1995) 'Managing Someone Else's Classroom During Student Teaching', in Slick, G. (ed.) *Making the Difference for Teachers* Thousand Oaks: Corwin.

Korthagen, F. and Wubbels, T. (1995) 'Characteristics of Reflective Practitioners: Towards an Operationalisation of the Concept of Reflection', *Teachers and Teaching: Theory and Practice*, 1 (1), 51–72.

Labaree, D. (1995) 'A Disabling Vision: Rhetoric and Reality in "Tomorrow's Schools of Education"', *Teachers College Record*, 97 (Winter), 166–205.

Lawlor, S. (1990) *Teachers Mistaught* London: Centre for Policy Studies.

Lawton, D. (1994) *The Tory Mind in Education 1974–1994* London: Falmer Press.

Lucas, P. (1991) 'Reflection, New Practices and the Need for Flexibility in Supervising Student Teachers', *Journal of Further and Higher Education*, 15 (2), 84–93.

McIntyre, A. (1981) *After Virtue* Notre Dame: Notre Dame Press.

McIntyre, A. (1985) 'The Idea of an Educated Public', in *Education and Values: The Richard Peters Lectures* London: Institute of Education.

McIntyre, D. (1993) 'Theory, Theorizing and Reflection in Initial Teacher Education', in Calderhead, J. and Gates, P. (eds) *Conceptualising Reflection in Teacher Development* London: Falmer Press.

McIntyre, D. and Hagger, H. (ed.) (1996) *Mentors in Schools: Developing the Profession of Teaching* London: Fulton.

McIntyre, D., Hagger, H. and Wilkin, M. (eds) (1993) *Mentoring: Perspectives on School-Based Teacher Education* London: Kogan Page.

McLaughlin, T. H. (1994) 'Values Coherence and the School', *Cambridge Journal of Education*, 24 (3), 453–470.

McLaughlin, T. (1996) 'Beyond the Reflective Teacher', Unpublished Paper, Cambridge University Department of Education.

Mardle, G. (1995) 'The Consequences', in Glover, D. and Mardle, G. (eds) *The Management of Mentoring* London: Kogan Page.

Moon, B. and Shelton Mayes, A. (1995) 'Integrating Values into the Assessment of Teachers in Initial Education and Training', in Kerry, T. and Shelton Mayes, A. (eds) *Issues in Mentoring* London: Routledge.

National Commission on Excellence in Education (1983) *A Nation at Risk*.

National Curriculum Council (NCC) (1990) *Curriculum Guidance No. 8: Education for Citizenship* London: NCC.

NCC (1993) *Spiritual and Moral Development* London: NCC.

National Council for Vocational Qualifications (NCVQ) (1989) *National Vocational Qualifications: Criteria and Procedures* London: NCVQ.

Naylor, F. (1996) 'Need to Clear the Fog around Values', *Times Educational Supplement*, 5 July.

Neville, S. (1993) 'Shared Values', in Selmes, C.S.G. and Robb, W.M. (eds) *Values and the Curriculum: Theory and Practice* London: National Association of Values in Education and Training.

Norris, N. (1991) 'The Trouble with Competence', *Cambridge Journal of Education*, 21 (3), 331–341.

Office for Standards in Education (OFSTED) (1993) *Handbook for the Inspection of Schools* Office for Standards in Education, London: HMSO.

OFSTED (1995) *The Annual Report of HM Chief Inspector of Schools 1994/95* Office for Standards in Education, London: HMSO.

OFSTED (1996) *The Appraisal of Teachers 1991–1996* Office for Standards in Education, London: HMSO.

O'Hear, A. (1988) *Who Teaches the Teachers?* Research Report No. 10 London: The Social Affairs Unit.

O'Neill, C., Lambert, A., Linnell, R. and Warr-Wood, J. (1977) *Drama Guidelines* London: Heinemann.

Parker, S. (1993) *The Craft of Writing* London: Paul Chapman.

Pring, R.A. (1992) 'Academic Respectability and Professional Relevance', Inaugural lecture delivered before the University of Oxford on 8 May 1991, Oxford: Clarendon Press.

Quicke, J. (1996) 'The Reflective Practitioner and Teacher Education: An Answer to Critics', *Teachers and Teaching: Theory and Practice*, 2 (1), 11–22.

Reid, D. (1994) 'Towards Empowerment: An Approach to School-Based Mentoring', in Field, B. and Field, T. (eds) *Teachers as Mentors: A Practical Guide* London: Falmer Press.

Ribich, F. (1995) 'Providing Meaningful Field Experiences', in Slick, G. (ed.) *The Field Experience* Thousand Oaks: Corwin.

Robinson, M. (1994) 'The Mentoring Scheme of Warwick University and Its School Partners – One Year On', in Field, B. and Field, T. (eds) *Teachers as Mentors: A Practical Guide* London: Falmer Press.

Rudduck, J. (1991) 'The Language of Consciousness and the Landscape of Action: Tensions in Teacher Education', *British Educational Research Journal*, 17 (4), 319–331.

Rutter, M., Maughan, B., Mortimer, P. and Ouston, J. (1979) *Fifteen Thousand Hours: Secondary Schools and Their Effects on Children* Wells: Open Books.

Sanders, S. (1994) 'Mathematics and Mentoring', in Jaworski, B. and Watson, A. (eds) *Mentoring in Mathematics Teaching* London: Falmer Press.

Schön, D. (1983) *The Reflective Practitioner* London: Temple Smith.

Schön, D. (1987) *Educating the Reflective Practitioner* San Francisco: Jossey-Bass.

Schools Curriculum and Assessment Authority (SCAA) (1996) Unpublished Working Papers for the National Forum for Values in Education and the Community, including a commissioned MORI poll, London: SCAA.

Scottish Office Education Department (SOED) (1993a) *Guidelines for Teacher Training Courses* Edinburgh: SOED.

SOED (1993b) *Report of the SOED Seminar on Partnership in Initial Teacher Training* Edinburgh: SOED.

SOED (1994a) Press Release, 'Mentor Teacher Scheme for Teacher Training', 12 May 1994, Edinburgh: SOED.

SOED (1994b) Press Release, 'Extra 2 Million for Mentor Training Scheme', 8 December 1994, Edinburgh: SOED.

SOED (1995a) 'Letter to All Headteachers of Secondary Schools' dated April 1995, Edinburgh: SOED.

SOED (1995b) Press Release, 'Mentor Scheme for Teacher Training Postponed for One Year', 21 July 1995, Edinburgh: SOED.

SOED (1995c) Press Release, 'Mentor Scheme Dropped in Favour of Improved Partnership between Schools and Teacher Institutions', 25 October 1995, Edinburgh: SOED.

Shulman, L. (1987) 'Knowledge and Teaching: Foundations of the New Reform', *Harvard Educational Review*, 57, 1–22.

Slick, G. (ed.) (1995a) *The Field Experience* Thousand Oaks: Corwin.

Slick, G. (ed.) (1995b) *Preparing New Teachers* Thousand Oaks: Corwin.

Smith, R. and Alred, G. (1993) 'The Impersonation of Wisdom', in McIntyre, D., Hagger, H. and Wilkin, M. (eds) *Mentoring: Perspectives on School-Based Teacher Education* London: Kogan Page.

Sockett, H. (1993) *The Moral Base for Teacher Professionalism* New York: Teachers College Press.

Stark, R. (1994) 'The "Giving" Can't Go On', *Times Educational Supplement Scotland*, 18 February.

Stephens, P. (1996) *Essential Mentoring Skills: A Practical Handbook for School-Based Teacher Educators* Cheltenham: Stanley Thorne.

Strain, M. (1995) 'Teaching as a Profession: The Changing Legal and Social Context', in Busher, H. and Saran, R. (eds) *Managing Teachers as Professionals in Schools* London: Kogan Page.

Strike, K.A. (1995) 'The Moral Responsibilities of Educators', in Sikula, J. (ed.) *Handbook of Research on Teacher Education* New York: Macmillan.

Stromach, I., Cope, P., Inglis, B. and McNally, J. (1994) 'The SOED Competence Guidelines for Initial Teacher Training: Issues of Control, Performance and Relevance', *Scottish Educational Review*, 26 (2), 118–133.

Stubbs, M. (1983) *Discourse Analysis* London: Basil Blackwell.

REFERENCES

Tabachnick, B.R. and Zeichner, K. (eds) (1991) *Issues and Practices in Inquiry-Oriented Teacher Education* London: Falmer Press.

Teacher Training Agency (TTA) (1996a) *Effective Training through Partnership: Working Papers on Secondary Partnership* London: TTA.

TTA (1996b) *Career Entry Profiles for Newly Qualified Secondary Teachers* London: TTA.

TTA (1996c) *Effective Training Through Partnership*, Four Working Papers, London: TTA.

TTA (1996d) *Quality of Teaching and Assessment* London: TTA.

TTA (1996e) News, 'Twin Boost for Teacher Training Reforms', *TTA* 27/96, 18 September.

Tickle, L. (1992) 'Professional Skills Assessment in Classroom Teaching', *Cambridge Journal of Education*, 22 (1), 91–103.

Tickle, L. (1996) 'Reflective Teaching: Embrace or Illusion?', in McBride, R. (ed.) *Teacher Education Policy: Some Issues Arising from Research and Practice* London: Falmer Press.

Tom, A.R. (1980) 'Teaching as a Moral Craft: A Metaphor for Teaching Teacher Education', *Curriculum Enquiry*, 10 (3), 317–323.

Tomlinson, P. (1995a) 'Can Competence Profiling Work for Effective Teacher Preparation? Part I General Issues', *Oxford Review of Education*, 21 (2), 179–194.

Tomlinson, P. (1995b) *Understanding Mentoring* Buckingham: Open University Press.

Watkins, C. and Whalley, C. (1993) *Mentoring: Resources for School-Based Development* Harlow: Longman

Watson, B. and Ashton, E. (1995) *Education, Assumptions and Values* London: David Fulton.

Werner, P., Avila, L., Resta, V., Vanglar, V. and Curtin, P. (1995) 'Feedback Measure in Field Experience Programs', in Slick, G. (ed) *The Field Experience* Thousand Oaks: Corwin.

White, J. (1990) 'The Aims of Education', in Entwistle, N. (ed.) *Handbook of Educational Ideas and Practices* London: Routledge.

Whiting, C., Whitty, G., Furlong, J., Miles, S. and Barton, L. (1996) *Partnership in Initial Teacher Education: A Topography* Modes of Teacher Education Project, London: London University Institute of Education.

Whitty, G. (1992) 'Quality Control in Teacher Education', *British Journal of Educational Studies*, 40 (1), 38–50.

Whitty, G. and Willmott, E. (1991) 'Competence-Based Approaches to Teacher Education: Approaches and Issues', *Cambridge Journal of Education*, 21 (3), 309–318. Also in Kerry, T. and Shelton Mayes, A. (eds) (1995) *Issues in Mentoring* London: Routledge.

Wilkin, M. (ed.) (1992) *Mentoring in Schools* London: Kogan Page.

Wilkin, M. (1993) 'Initial Training as a Case of Postmodern Development: Some Implications for Mentoring', in McIntyre, D., Hagger, H. and Wilkin, M. (eds) *Mentoring: Perspectives on School-Based Teacher Education* London: Kogan Page.

Wilkin, M. (1996) *Initial Teacher Training: The Dialogue of Ideology and Culture* London: Falmer Press.

REFERENCES

Williams, A., Butterfield, S., Gray, C., Leach, S., Marr, A. and Soare, A. (1996) 'Form, Function and Focus in Mentor Student Dialogue within a Secondary Initial Teacher Education Partnership', Paper presented to Exploring Futures in Initial Teacher Education, Institute of Education, University of London, September.

Wilson, J. (1993) *Reflections and Practice: Teacher Education and the Teaching Profession* University of Western Ontario: Althouse Press.

Wilson, J. (1996) 'An Evaluation of the Field Experiences of the Innovative Model for the Preparation of Elementary Teachers for Science, Mathematics and Technology', *Journal of Teacher Education*, 47 (Jan/Feb), 53–59.

Wilson, S. and Wineburg, S. (1991) 'Wrinkles in Time and Place: Using Performance Indicators to Understand the Knowledge of History Teachers', Paper presented at the Annual Meeting of the American Educational Research Association, Boston. Cited in John, P. (1994) 'The Integration of Research Validated Knowledge with Practice', *Cambridge Journal of Education*, 24 (1), 33–47.

Zeichner, K. (1983) 'Alternative Paradigms of Teacher Education', *Journal of Teacher Education*, 34 (3), 3–9.

Zeichner, K. (1990) 'Changing Directions in the Practicum: Looking Ahead to the 1990s', *Journal of Education for Teaching*, 16 (2), 105–132.

Zeichner, K. (1993) 'Traditions of Practice in U.S. Preservice Teacher Education Programs', *Teaching and Teacher Education*, 9 (1), 1–13.

Zeichner, K. (1994) 'Research on Teacher Thinking and Different Views of Reflective Practice in Teaching and Teacher Education', in Carlgen, I., Handal, G. and Vaage, S. (eds) *Teachers' Minds and Actions: Research on Teachers' Thinking and Practice* London: Falmer Press.

Zeichner, K. and Liston, D. (1985) 'Varieties of Discourse in Supervisory Conferences', *Teaching and Teacher Education*, 1, 155–174.

165

INDEX